The Hulton Getty Picture Collection

1940s

Decades of the 20th Century
Décadas del siglo XX
Decadi del XX secolo

GW00545361

The Hulton Getty Picture Collection
1940s

Decades of the 20th Century
Décadas del siglo XX
Decadi del XX secolo

Nick Yapp

KÖNEMANN

The trilingual edition in English, French and German first published in 1998 by Könemann Verlagsgesellschaft mbH, Bonner Straße 126, D-50968 Köln

This book was produced by The Hulton Getty Picture Collection Limited, Unique House, 21–31 Woodfield Road, London W9 2BA

For Könemann:
Managing editor: Sally Bald
Project editor: Susanne Hergarden

For Hulton Getty: Editor: James Hughes
Art director: Michael Rand Proof reader: Elisabeth Ihre
Design: Ian Denning Scanning: Paul Wright
Managing editor: Annabel Else Production: Robert Gray
Picture editor: Ali Khoja Special thanks: Leon Meyer,
Picture research: Alex Linghorn Téa Aganovic and Antonia Hille

Colour separation by Jade Reprographics Ltd.

© 2000 for the trilingual edition in English, Spanish and Italian:
Könemann Verlagsgesellschaft mbH
Spanish translation: David Egea Oriol for LocTeam, S.L., Barcelona
Italian translation: Gabriele Miccichè for Ready-made, Milan
Typesetting: Ready-made, Milan

Project editors: Anabel Martín Encinas, Alessandra Provenzano
Production: Mark Voges
Printed and bound: Star Standard Industries Ltd

ISBN 3-8290-6174-9

10 9 8 7 6 5 4 3 2 1

Frontispiece: 'When Jenny comes marching home…' The war is over, and a servicewoman is greeted by her mother and family on her 'demob' from the Women's Auxiliary Air Force. 10 September 1945.

Frontispicio: "Cuando Jenny vuelva a casa..." La guerra había terminado. Tras la desmovilización, una auxiliar del ejército femenino del aire regresa a casa, donde le dan la bienvenida su madre y su familia, el 10 de septiembre de 1945.

Frontespizio : "Jenny torna a casa..." La guerra è finita e un'ausiliaria dell'esercito è accolta dalla madre e dalla famiglia dopo la smobilitazione. 10 settembre 1945.

Contents / Contenido / Sommario

Introduction

More than any other decade in the century, the 1940s were split down the middle. All was war and destruction until 1945. A good deal was post-war reconstruction thereafter. It was a time when everything was in short supply – except arms and ammunition. For most of the decade, people lived in the dark, deprived of electricity, the truth, food, clothes and any semblance of comfort. In war and peace, they ate what they could get: horse, whale meat, dried egg, ersatz coffee made of acorns, rats and spam.

For five long, desperate years large chunks of the world were battlegrounds – in Europe, North Africa, the Pacific and the Atlantic, Burma, China, the Philippines, and vast swathes of the Soviet Union. People fought for freedom, dug for victory, prayed for liberation. It was an age of heroism and brutality, of triumph and suffering, of bravery and cowardice (not all of it during the war), of determination in the best and worst of causes. And it was a decade that was to produce three almighty hangovers: the Holocaust, the Bomb and the Cold War.

When the fighting at last stopped, whole populations searched and scratched about them – looking for their homes, their families, work, a meaning for life, and a reason for living. For some there was the excitement of being part of a new nation, in Israel, India, Pakistan and Communist China.

By and large, escapism was hard to come by. After the war, the circus came back to town. Sport returned, with record gates at football, cricket and baseball games. Australian cricket maestro Don Bradman bowed out at the Oval. Stanley Matthews, footballing genius, wove his magic at Wembley. Joe Louis floored his opponents wherever he came across them. Gorgeous Gussie Moran brought sex to tennis. The New York Yankees won two of the four post-war baseball World Series.

Fashion had a bumpy ride. Until 1945, it was fashionable to be in uniform. Civilian suits and dresses were subject to restrictions on both the quantity and quality of material used. Clothes, like so many other things were 'rationed'. But when the fighting stopped, along came Christian Dior and others with the New Look, a return to the sumptuous.

There was a whole new glossary of words spawned by the war: 'blitz', 'evacuee', 'GI', 'Home Guard', 'jeep', 'pontoon bridge', 'lend lease'. With the coming of peace, new words emerged: 'prefab', 'demob', 'nylon'. Anne Frank's diary was published. George Orwell wrote *Animal Farm* and *1984*. Bertrand Russell wrote *A History of Western Philosophy*. Gandhi was asked what he thought of Western civilization. 'I think,' he said, 'it would be a very good idea.'

Aviator Amy Johnson and musician Glenn Miller disappeared. Film stars Jane Russell and Frank Sinatra arrived. *Casablanca* became famous as a film. Casablanca became famous as the meeting place of Churchill, Roosevelt and de Gaulle. Four boys stumbled upon the prehistoric painted caves of Lascaux. Hundreds of scientists unlocked the secret of splitting the atom.

And the United Nations brought new hope for the future.

Introducción

De manera más drástica que ninguna otra década del siglo, los años cuarenta estuvieron divididos en dos mitades. Hasta 1945 todo fue guerra y destrucción. Después tuvo que reconstruirse de nuevo la civilización. Fue una época en la que faltaba de todo, excepto armas y munición. Durante la mayor parte de la década, la gente vivió en la oscuridad, sin electricidad, sin conocer la verdad de lo que estaba ocurriendo, sin comida ni ropa y sin ninguna de las comodidades de antaño. Tanto en tiempo de guerra como de paz, la gente comía lo que podía: carne de caballo o de ballena, huevos en polvo, sucedáneo de café hecho a partir de bellotas, ratas o carne de cerdo enlatada.

Durante cinco largos y angustiosos años, vastas regiones del planeta fueron campos de batalla, en Europa, el norte de África, el Pacífico y el Atlántico, Birmania, China, Filipinas y gran parte de la Unión Soviética. La gente luchaba por la libertad, cavaba trincheras para la victoria y rezaba por la liberación. Fue una época de heroísmo y brutalidad, de triunfo y sufrimiento, de coraje y cobardía, aunque no solo durante la guerra, y de decisiones firmes tanto para las mejores como para las peores causas. Pero también fue una década que engendró tres importantes fenómenos históricos: el Holocausto, la bomba atómica y la guerra fría.

Cuando por fin cesaron las hostilidades, millones de personas se pusieron a buscar y escarbar entre los escombros tratando de hallar su casa, su familia, un trabajo, algún sentido a la vida y una razón para vivir. En el caso de algunos se añadía la emoción de formar parte de una nueva nación, como en Israel, India, Paquistán y la China comunista.

Tras la guerra, en general resultaba difícil evadirse de la dura realidad. La vida volvió a las ciudades, y con ella los deportes. Los encuentros de fútbol, críquet y béisbol registraban entradas récord. El gran jugador de críquet australiano Don Bradman eligió el estadio de Oval para retirarse. Stanley Matthews, un genio del fútbol, llevó su magia a Wembley. Joe Louis derrumbaba a sus oponentes en el cuadrilátero una y otra vez. La hermosa Gussie Moran trajo un poco de sabor femenino al tenis. El equipo de béisbol de los New York Yankees ganó dos de los cuatro campeonatos World Series celebrados después de la guerra.

La moda vivió momentos de agitación. Hasta 1945 estuvo de moda llevar uniforme. Los trajes y vestidos de la población civil sufrieron restricciones tanto en la cantidad como en la calidad del material utilizado en su confección. La ropa, como muchos otros artículos, también estaba racionada. Sin embargo, al finalizar la guerra, Christian Dior y otros diseñadores invadieron las tiendas con el New Look, que significó un retorno a la suntuosidad de épocas anteriores.

La guerra trajo una enorme cantidad de neologismos: *Blitz*, evacuado, GI, fuerza de reserva, jeep, puente de pontones, préstamo y arriendo. Con la paz llegaron también muchas palabras nuevas: prefabricado, desmovilización, nilón. Se publicó el diario de Ana Frank. George Orwell escribió *Rebelión en la granja* y *1984*. Bertrand Russell publicó *Historia de la filosofía occidental*. Gandhi expresó en una entrevista lo que pensaba de la civilización occidental: "Creo que sería una muy buena idea".

La aviadora Amy Johnson y el músico Glenn Miller desaparecieron en el aire. Se dieron a conocer estrellas de cine como Jane Russell y Frank Sinatra. *Casablanca* se hizo famosa gracias al largometraje homónimo, así como por ser un lugar de reunión de Churchill, Roosevelt y De Gaulle. Cuatro chicos descubrieron por azar las cuevas prehistóricas de Lascaux. Centenares de científicos desvelaron el secreto de la fisión del átomo.

Finalmente, los cuarenta fueron también la década en que la Organización de las Naciones Unidas trajo una nueva esperanza para el futuro.

Introduzione

Più di ogni altro decennio gli anni Quaranta si dividono in due parti nettamente distinte. Fino al 1945 tutto è guerra e distruzione, cui seguirà però un grandioso periodo di ricostruzione. Furono anni in cui scarseggiava tutto, eccetto le armi e le munizioni. Per la maggior parte del decennio la gente visse nell'oscurità, priva di elettricità, di cibo, di vestiario e di ogni apparenza di benessere. Sia in guerra che in pace si mangiava ciò che si trovava: carne di cavallo o di balena, uova liofilizzate, surrogato di caffè fatto con ghiande, ratti, succedanei della carne.

Per cinque lunghi, disperati anni ampie parti del mondo intero si trasformarono in campi di battaglia: in Europa e Nord Africa, dal Pacifico all'Atlantico, in Birmania, Cina, nelle Filippine, oltre che in gran parte dell'Unione Sovietica. La gente combatteva per la libertà, lavorava per la vittoria, pregava per la liberazione. Fu un'epoca di eroismo e brutalità, di trionfi e sofferenze, di coraggio e viltà (e non solamente nei campi di battaglia), di determinazione nelle migliori e nelle peggiori cause. E fu un decennio che produsse tre fatti indelebili: l'Olocausto, la Bomba atomica e la Guerra fredda.

Quando alla fine la guerra si ferma, intere popolazioni sono alla ricerca di se stesse: alla ricerca delle loro case, delle loro famiglie, di lavoro, del significato della vita, di una ragione per vivere. Per alcune di esse comincia l'eccitante esperienza di appartenere a una nuova nazione: in Israele, India, Pakistan e nella Cina comunista.

Nel complesso è difficile trovare un diversivo, ma presto la vita torna alla normalità. Lo sport ritorna con nuovi record di affluenza nel calcio, nel cricket e nel baseball. Il campione australiano di cricket Don Bradman gioca all'Oval, il leggendario campo di Londra. Stanley Mattews, il geniale calciatore, affascina le folle di Wembley. Joe Louis sbaraglia gli avversari che osano sfidarlo. Il fascinoso Gussie Moran dà un tocco di seduzione al tennis. Gli Yankees di New York vincono due dei quattro campionati del mondo di baseball del dopoguerra.

Per la moda comincia un periodo inquieto. Fino al 1945 era *à la page* portare l'uniforme. I vestiti da civile subivano restrizioni tanto nella quantità quanto nella qualità dei materiali usati. Gli abiti, come quasi tutto il resto, erano razionati. Ma alla fine delle ostilità, con il New Look, Christian Dior e altri stilisti riportarono in auge il lusso.

Si inaugura un glossario tutto nuovo di neologismi introdotti dalla guerra: 'blitz', 'evacuato', 'GI', 'territoriale', 'jeep', 'ponte di barche', 'leasing'. Ma emergono anche nuove parole di pace: 'prefabbricato', 'smobilitazione', 'nylon'. Si pubblica il *Diario* di Anna Frank, Orwell scrive *La fattoria degli animali* e *1984*. Bertrand Russell pubblica la *Storia della filosofia occidentale*. Gandhi alla domanda su cosa pensasse della civiltà occidentale risponde: "Sarebbe un'ottima idea".

Scompaiono l'aviatore Amy Johnson e il musicista Glenn Miller. Emergono le star Jane Russell e Frank Sinatra. *Casablanca* diventa un film di culto, e la città diventa celebre anche come sede dell'incontro tra Churchill, Roosevelt e De Gaulle. Quattro ragazzini scoprono per caso le pitture rupestri preistoriche a Lascaux. Centinaia di fisici scoprono il segreto della fissione atomica.

E le Nazioni Unite fanno nascere una nuova speranza per il futuro.

1. Total war
Guerra total
Guerra totale

A US infantryman stands guard over a beachhead on the Pacific island of Okinawa in 1945. The coral reef in the background has been dynamited to prepare a landing place for American supply ships.

Un soldado de infantería estadounidense monta guardia en una playa de la isla de Okinawa, en el Pacífico, en 1945. El arrecife de coral que aparece al fondo ha sido dinamitado para utilizarlo como lugar de desembarco de los barcos de suministro.

Un soldato americano monta la guardia sull'altura di una spiaggia dell'isola di Okinawa, nel Pacifico, 1945. La barriera corallina alle sue spalle è stata bombardata per preparare un approdo adatto ai mezzi di sbarco americani sulla spiaggia.

1. Total war
Guerra total
Guerra totale

When Churchill growled of fighting on the seas and oceans, on the beaches, on the landing grounds, in the fields, in the streets, and in the hills, he knew what he was talking about, though it didn't all come to pass in Britain.

World War II savaged people's lives in a way no other had. The Soviet Union suffered most in terms of casualties. Germany and Japan suffered most in terms of destruction and the misery of defeat. If ever proof was needed of the waste and stupidity of war in general, this war specifically provided it.

And yet few doubted that it had to be fought, and with every weapon available. The stakes were high. On the one side was a Reich boasting it would last 1,000 years. On the other, old empires and new democracies somehow glued together.

Graveyards sprang up all over the world: in the Pacific, the Atlantic, North Africa, the whole of Europe, the Far East, even in a South American river mouth. You could be killed thousands of miles from home or in your own backyard. Death came hurtling from the clouds, slinking from under the sea, and scorching across the earth. In all, some 50 million people were killed in the war.

Cuando Churchill declaró enfadado que la lucha se extendería por mares y océanos, playas, aeropuertos, calles, campos y montañas, sabía de qué estaba hablando, aunque Reino Unido no iba a ser el único escenario de la contienda.

La Segunda Guerra Mundial alteró la vida de las personas como ninguna otra guerra antes. La Unión Soviética fue el país que más vidas humanas perdió. Alemania y Japón fueron los que más sufrieron en términos de destrucción, miseria y derrota. Si fuera necesario demostrar lo estúpidas e inútiles que son las guerras, ésta sería perfecta para hacerlo.

Sin embargo, pocos dudaron de la necesidad de luchar, y con todas las armas posibles. Las apuestas eran elevadas. Por un lado, un Reich que proclamaba que duraría 1.000 años. Por el otro, viejos imperios y nuevas democracias que, ante la situación, se vieron obligados a encontrar la manera de colaborar.

Los cementerios se multiplicaron en número por todo el mundo: en el Pacífico, en el Atlántico, en el norte de África, en toda Europa, en Extremo Oriente, incluso en el estuario de un río de América del Sur. A uno podían matarle tanto a miles de kilómetros de casa como en el propio jardín. La muerte aparecía súbitamente de entre las nubes, se deslizaba furtivamente bajo el mar y devastaba los campos. En total, la guerra se cobró aproximadamente 50 millones de víctimas.

Quando Churchill proclamò una guerra sui mari e sugli oceani, sulle spiagge, sulla terraferma, nei campi, per le strade, nelle colline, sapeva bene di cosa stava parlando, anche se forse non tutta la Gran Bretagna lo capì.

La seconda guerra mondiale brutalizzò la vita della gente in un modo mai visto prima. L'Unione Sovietica contò il maggior numero di vittime. Germania e Giappone le maggiori distruzioni, soffrendo poi la miseria dovuta alla sconfitta. Se c'era bisogno di provare la stupidità della guerra in generale, questa guerra lo fece senza ombra di dubbio.

Eppure pochi dubitarono che essa andava combattuta con tutte le armi disponibili. La posta in gioco era altissima. Da un lato c'era un Reich che ambiva a una durata millenaria. Dall'altra vecchi imperi e nuove democrazie che si dovettero alleare per forza di cose.

I cimiteri si moltiplicarono in tutto il mondo: nel Pacifico, nell'Atlantico, in Nord Africa, in tutta l'Europa, nell'Estremo Oriente e persino nell'estuario di un fiume del Sud America. Si poteva morire a migliaia di chilometri da casa o nel proprio giardino. La morte si abbatteva dal cielo o si insinuava furtivamente da sotto i mari o emergeva dalla terra stessa. In totale, almeno 50 milioni di persone persero la vita.

Hitler and Marshal of the Reich Hermann Göring take time out from the disasters of 1942. Two years later Göring was in disgrace.

Hitler y el mariscal del Reich Hermann Göring hablan acerca de los desastres de 1942. Dos años más tarde, Göring cayó en desgracia ante Hitler.

Hitler e il maresciallo del Reich Hermann Göring discutono delle catastrofi del 1942. Due anni più tardi, Göring cadde in disgrazia.

A Cherbourg docker lights Churchill's cigar. Churchill was visiting what was left of the French port in June 1944, just a few days after the D-day landings. The town suffered a week-long siege before it was liberated.

Un estibador de Cherburgo enciende el cigarro de Churchill, que estaba realizando una visita a lo que quedaba de este puerto francés en junio de 1944, sólo unos días después del desembarco del día D. Antes de ser liberada, la ciudad estuvo sitiada durante una semana.

Un portuale di Cherbourg accende il sigaro di Churchill. Churchill sta visitando ciò che resta del porto francese nel giugno 1944, pochi giorni dopo lo sbarco del D-day. La città aveva sofferto una settimana di assedio prima di essere liberata.

Disaster at Dieppe. Canadian survivors of an ill-planned attack on Dieppe return to Britain, August 1942. They lost half their comrades. The raid was an ill-conceived rehearsal for D-day two years later.

Desastre en Dieppe. Supervivientes canadienses de un ataque mal planeado contra Dieppe regresan al Reino Unido, en agosto de 1942. Perdieron a la mitad de sus camaradas. El ataque fue un intento fallido de día D, que tendría lugar dos años más tarde.

Disastro a Dieppe. Alcuni canadesi sopravvissuti all'attacco mal preparato contro Dieppe ritornano in Gran Bretagna nell'agosto 1942. Hanno perso la metà dei loro compagni. Il raid fu una prova generale, malamente organizzata, del D-day di due anni più tardi.

Disaster at Dunkirk. The French destroyer *Bourrasque* sinks off the Dunkirk beaches during the withdrawal of Allied troops. While they were being loaded with their human cargo, ships like these were sitting targets for German planes.

Desastre en Dunquerque. El destructor francés *Bourrasque* se hunde cerca de las costas de Dunquerque durante la retirada de las tropas aliadas. Mientras la tripulación embarcaba, los barcos como éste eran un blanco fácil para la aviación alemana.

Disastro a Dunkerque. Il cacciatorpediniere francese *Bourrasque* affonda al largo della spiaggia di Dunkerque durante il ritiro delle truppe alleate. Mentre trasportavano il loro carico umano, navi come questa erano alla mercè dell'aviazione tedesca.

Free French. In June 1940, General Charles de Gaulle delivers the speech in which he called on his countrymen and women to continue the fight against Germany, even though France had fallen, and he was himself in exile.

Objetivo: liberar Francia. En junio de 1940, el general Charles de Gaulle pronuncia un discurso en el que pide a sus compatriotas que sigan luchando contra Alemania aunque Francia haya caído y él mismo se encuentre en el exilio.

Liberare la Francia. Il generale Charles de Gaulle pronuncia il celebre discorso in cui esorta i suoi compatrioti, uomini e donne, a continuare la lotta contro la Germania anche se la Francia è sconfitta e lui stesso si trova in esilio.

Vichy French. Premier Pierre Laval (right) and Marshal Henri Philippe Pétain in 1940. In their collaborationist France, 'Liberty, Equality, Fraternity' was replaced by 'Work, Family and Fatherland'.

Vichy. El primer ministro Pierre Laval (derecha) y el mariscal Henri Philippe Pétain, en 1940. En su Francia colaboracionista, el lema "Libertad, igualdad, fraternidad" fue sustituido por "Trabajo, familia, patria".

Vichy. Il primo ministro Pierre Laval (a destra) e il maresciallo Henri Philippe Pétain, nel 1940. Nella loro Francia collaborazionista "Libertà, uguaglianza e fraternità" si trasforma in "Lavoro, famiglia e patria".

RAF pilots run to their planes on an alert at a Fleet Air Arm
Training Centre. The Battle of Britain was already over when
this picture was taken in 1943, but the 'scramble' went on.

Pilotos de la RAF corren hacia sus aviones en un simulacro
de alarma en un centro de entrenamiento de la aviación. La
Batalla de Inglaterra ya había terminado cuando se tomó esta
foto, pero los entrenamientos continuaban.

Piloti della RAF corrono verso gli aerei dopo un allarme in
un campo di addestramento dell'aviazione militare. La
battaglia d'Inghilterra era già finita quando fu scattata questa
foto, nel 1943, ma l'addestramento proseguiva.

A lull in the fighting, a battle of wits. RAF pilots relax during the Battle of Britain in March 1940. The jacket and boots worn by the officer on the left suggests they were expecting an 'alert' at any moment.

Momentos de calma antes de la tormenta: táctica y estrategia sobre el tablero. Pilotos de la RAF descansan durante la Batalla de Inglaterra en marzo de 1940. La chaqueta y las botas que lleva el oficial de la izquierda indican que en cualquier momento puede producirse una alarma.

La calma prima della tempesta: rafforzare lo spirito. Piloti della RAF si riposano durante la battaglia d'Inghilterra. Il giaccone e gli stivali indossati dall'ufficiale sulla sinistra fanno presumere che essi aspettassero un allarme da un momento all'altro.

Easter 1940. British troops sample the delights of NAAFI hot cross buns. To some the Navy Army and Air Force Institutes was a godsend. To others it was a joke: NAAFI tea was even rumoured to lower a man's sex drive.

Pascua de 1940. Dos soldados británicos prueban los deliciosos panecillos de leche ligeramente picantes de los NAAFI. Para algunos, los Navy Army and Air Force Institutes eran como una bendición. Para otros, en cambio, era motivo de burla: se decía que el té de los NAAFI disminuía el apetito sexual masculino.

Pasqua del 1940. Soldati britannici gustano i deliziosi panini al latte dei NAAFI. Per alcuni i Navy Army and Air Force Institutes erano un dono di Dio. Per altri erano una trappola: si diceva che il tè dei NAAFI abbassasse il desiderio sessuale degli uomini.

October 1940. At the height of the Battle of Britain,
a coastal defence soldier primes Mills bombs.
The German invasion was expected at any time.

Octubre de 1940. En el punto álgido de la Batalla
de Inglaterra, un soldado de la guardia costera
prepara granadas. Se esperaba que la invasión
alemana se produjera de un momento a otro.

Ottobre 1940. All'apogeo della battaglia
d'Inghilterra un soldato della difesa costiera prepara
delle granate. Si temeva un'invasione dei tedeschi in
ogni momento.

Advancing to victory. Russian troops in Berlin, April 1945.
The war was almost over. One prominent Nazi, Albert Speer,
reckoned that was a good thing. 'It was just an opera,'
he said. For most Germans, this was *Götterdämmerung*.

Avanzando hacia la victoria. Soldados rusos en Berlín,
en abril de 1945. La guerra ya casi había terminado. Un
célebre nazi, Albert Speer, confesó que le había gustado.
"Fue tan sólo una ópera", afirmó. Para la mayoría de
alemanes fue *Götterdämmerung* (el ocaso de los dioses).

Avanzare fino alla vittoria. Truppe russe a Berlino nell'aprile
1945. La guerra è praticamente finita. Uno dei più noti
nazisti, Albert Speer, ammette che è una buona cosa. "È stata
soltanto un'opera" affermò. Per la maggior parte dei tedeschi
si trattò di un *Götterdämmerung* (Crepuscolo degli Dei).

Advancing to defeat. Exhausted German troops take a break on their push to Moscow, August 1941. They had just reached the town of Vitebsk, to find it deserted and ablaze – a scene they would find repeated in most Russian towns.

Avanzando hacia la derrota. Soldados alemanes exhaustos descansan un momento durante la ofensiva contra Moscú, en agosto de 1941. Acaban de tomar la ciudad de Vitebsk, que han encontrado desierta e incendiada, un escenario con el que se toparían repetidamente en muchas ciudades rusas.

Avanzare fino alla sconfitta. Truppe tedesche esauste si riposano durante l'offensiva verso Mosca nell'agosto 1941. Hanno appena raggiunto la città di Vitebsk trovandola desertra e incendiata: una scena che si sarebbe ripetuta spesso nella maggior parte delle città russe.

Frozen members of the German Wehrmacht on the
Eastern Front, 1942. Tens of thousands died of cold.
Food was scarce. Morale reached rock bottom. Within
a couple of months, the Wehrmacht was in retreat.

Soldados helados de frío de la Wehrmacht alemana
en el frente oriental, en 1942. Decenas de miles de
hombres murieron congelados. La comida era escasa.
La moral estaba por los suelos. Un par de meses más
tarde, la Wehrmacht se batía en retirada.

Soldati tedeschi della Wehrmacht congelati sul fronte
orientale nel 1942. Decine di migliaia morirono di
freddo. Il cibo era scarso. Il morale bassissimo.
Qualche mese più tardi la Wehrmacht comincia la
ritirata.

The 'Great Patriotic War', 1941. A wounded Russian officer urges his men forward. Losses and suffering on the Soviet side were appalling.

La "Gran guerra patriótica", en 1941. Un oficial ruso herido ordena a sus hombres que avancen. El número de bajas y el sufrimiento entre las filas rusas fueron terribles.

La " Grande guerra patriottica " del 1941. Un ufficiale russo ferito incita i suoi uomini ad avanzare. Le perdite e le sofferenze subite dai sovietici furono spaventose.

'A day which will live in infamy.' Explosions shatter
the Naval Air Station at Pearl Harbor on 7 December
1941. 'America was suddenly and deliberately attacked
by the Empire of Japan,' said Roosevelt.
'We will gain the inevitable triumph, so help us God.'

"Un día para los anales de la infamia". Varias
explosiones reducen a cenizas la base aérea de Pearl
Harbour, el 7 de diciembre de 1941. "EE.UU. ha sido
atacado sin avisar y deliberadamente por el imperio
japonés", declaró Roosevelt. "Vamos a ganar esta
guerra. ¡Que Dios nos ayude!"

" Un giorno che passerà alla storia come il giorno
dell'infamia ". Esplosioni scuotono la base aerea di
Pearl Harbour, il 7 dicembre 1941. " L'America è stata
attaccata senza preavviso e deliberatamente dall'impero
giapponese" dichiara il presidente Roosevelt.
"Riporteremo un trionfo inevitabile, che Dio ci aiuti."

Nearing the end in the West. An exhausted German trooper in Belgium, some months after the D-day landings.

El final está cerca en el frente occidental. En la foto, un soldado alemán exhausto en Bélgica, unos meses después del desembarco del día D.

La fine si avvicina all'Ovest. Un soldato tedesco esausto in Belgio, pochi mesi dopo il D-day.

First strike in the East. A Japanese pilot completes his ceremonial dress before setting out to bomb Pearl Harbor.

Primera ofensiva en el frente oriental. Un piloto japonés realizando el típico ritual de colocarse un pañuelo en la cabeza, momentos antes de partir hacia Pearl Harbour.

Prima offensiva all'Est. Un pilota giapponese completa il cerimoniale di vestizione prima del decollo per il bombardamento di Pearl Harbour.

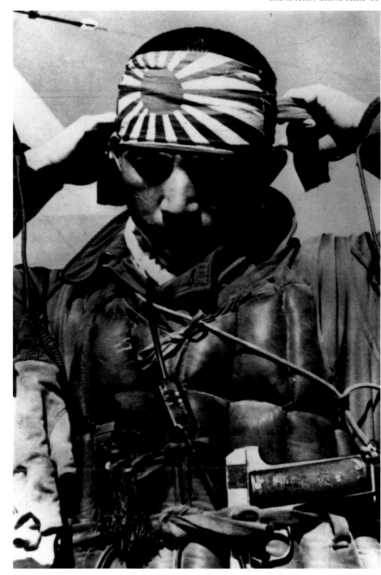

October 1942. The first black servicewomen from the United States arrive in Britain. About half a million blacks served overseas in segregated units.

Octubre de 1942. Las primeras mujeres militares de raza negra de EE.UU. llegan al Reino Unido. Más de medio millón de personas de esta raza participaron en la guerra en unidades separadas de los de raza blanca.

Ottobre 1942. Le prime donne militari di colore degli Stati Uniti arrivano in Gran Bretagna. Più di mezzo milione di persone di colore servirono oltremare in unità separate.

September 1942. Corporal Raymond Du Pont plays a hymn on a portable harmonium somewhere in Britain. Although discrimination persisted in the US Army, black troops were given a warm welcome by local civilians.

Septiembre de 1942. El caporal Raymond Du Pont interpreta un himno con un armonio portátil en algún lugar del Reino Unido. Aunque la discriminación racial continuó en el ejército estadounidense, los soldados de raza negra recibieron una cálida acogida entre los ciudadanos británicos.

Settembre 1942. Il caporale Raymond Du Pont suona un inno all'harmonium portatile da qualche parte in Gran Bretagna. Anche se esisteva la discriminazione all'interno dell'esercito americano, i soldati di colore vennero accolti dai civili calorosamente.

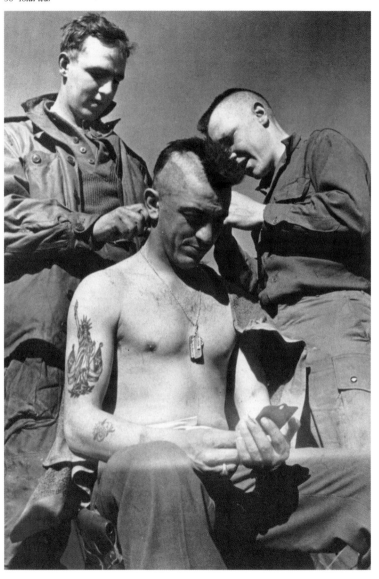

Heads… US paratroopers get a 'Comanche' haircut in March 1945. The next day, they parachuted down six miles east of the Rhine.

De la cabeza… Paracaidistas estadounidenses se cortan el pelo al estilo "comanche", en marzo de 1945. Al día siguiente se lanzaron en paracaídas desde una altura de diez kilómetros al este del Rin.

Dalla testa… Paracadutisti americani si tagliano i capelli alla "comanche" nel marzo 1945. Il giorno seguente si paracaduteranno a una decina di chilometri a est del Reno.

Toes... Regular foot inspection was essential for British soldiers of the 7th Armoured Division (the Desert Rats) as they fought their way across North Africa.

...a los pies. La inspección regular de los pies era esencial para los soldados británicos de la 7.ª División Acorazada (las Ratas del Desierto) durante su ofensiva en el norte de África.

... ai piedi! L'ispezione regolamentare dei piedi era essenziale per i soldati britannici della VII divisione blindata (i Desert Rats) durante l'offensiva in Nord Africa.

A Liberator bomber drops its load on Ploiesti in 1944. Ploiesti was in the heart of the Romanian oil fields, Hitler's major source of supply.

Un bombardero estadounidense Liberator arroja bombas sobre Ploiesti, en 1944. Situada en el corazón de la zona petrolífera de Rumania, la ciudad de Ploiesti era la principal fuente de suministro de Hitler.

Un bombardiere Liberator lancia il suo carico su Ploiesti nel 1944. Nel cuore dei campi pertoliferi rumeni, Ploiesti era la principale fonte di approvvigionamento di Hitler.

500-pound bombs from a Flying Fortress hurtle toward the oil refinery at Livorno (Leghorn), Italy, towards the end of the war.

Bombas de 500 libras caen desde una fortaleza volante sobre la refinería de petróleo de Livorno, en Italia, hacia el final de la guerra.

Bombe da 500 libbre lanciate da una fortezza volante piombano sulla raffineria di petrolio di Livorno verso la fine della guerra.

Jewish deportees arriving at Auschwitz, Poland, in 1940.
Of all the infamous concentration camps, Auschwitz was
perhaps the worst. It is unlikely that any of the people
in this photograph survived the war.

Judíos deportados llegan a Auschwitz, Polonia en 1940.
De todos los campos de concentración, Auschwitz fue
quizás el peor. Es muy probable que ninguna de las
personas de la foto lograra sobrevivir.

Deportati ebrei arrivano ad Auschwitz, in Polonia, nel
1940. Di tutti i tremendi campi di concentramento,
Auschwitz fu forse il peggiore. È molto improbabile che
qualcuno ritratto in questa fotografia sia sopravvissuto
alla guerra.

German civilian prisoners captured by Polish patriots in Warsaw, August 1944. The Poles rose against German occupying troops, believing that the Russians were only a few days' fighting away. But no help came, and the rising was brutally crushed.

Civiles alemanes capturados por patriotas polacos en Varsovia, en agosto de 1944. Los polacos se sublevaron contra las tropas de ocupación alemanas creyendo que los rusos entrarían en la ciudad a los pocos días, pero nadie vino en su ayuda y el levantamiento fue aplastado brutalmente.

Civili tedeschi fatti prigionieri dalla resistenza polacca a Varsavia, agosto 1944. I polacchi si sollevarono contro le truppe tedesche d'invasione convinti che i russi fossero soltanto a pochi giorni di combattimento. Ma non era così e il tentativo fu brutalmente soffocato nel sangue.

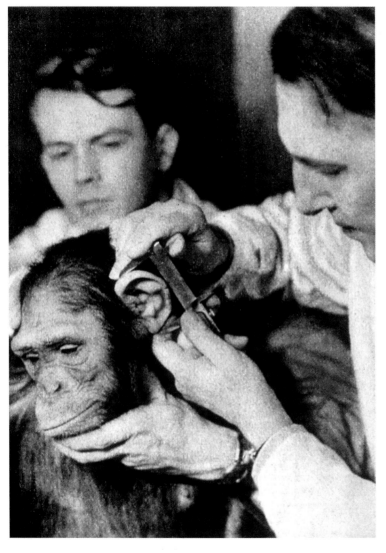

German zoologists chart the process of evolution, 1940. The ape will be better treated than millions of human beings.

Zoólogos alemanes estudian el proceso evolutivo, en 1940. Los chimpancés recibían un trato mejor que el de millones de seres humanos.

Zoologi tedeschi studiano il processo evolutivo, 1940. La scimmia riceverà un trattamento migliore di molti milioni di esseri umani.

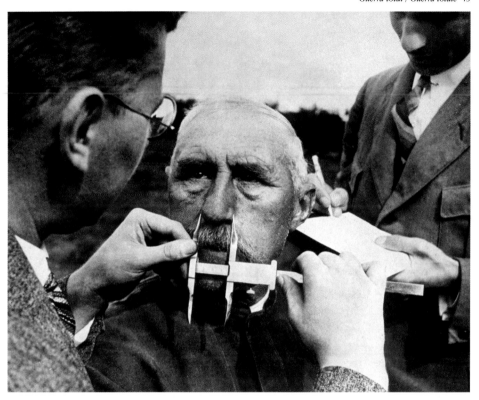

At the height of Nazi persecution of the Jews, an old man's physiognomy is measured by investigators. In some cases the fate of a subject depended on the measurements of his or her features.

En el momento álgido de la persecución nazi contra los judíos, unos inspectores estudian la fisionomía de un anciano. En algunos casos, la suerte de las personas dependía de las medidas de sus facciones.

Al culmine della persecuzione nazista degli ebrei, la fisionomia di un vecchio viene studiata da alcuni ispettori. In alcuni casi il destino di una persona poteva dipendere dalle misure dei suoi lineamenti.

Jewish civilians from the Warsaw ghetto surrender to German soldiers in 1943. Of the 600,000 Jews who were confined there, only 60,000 survived – among them the young boy in the foreground of this picture. Most of the others perished in the death camps.

Civiles judíos del gueto de Varsovia se rinden a los soldados alemanes en 1943. De los 600.000 judíos allí confinados, sólo 60.000 lograron sobrevivir, entre ellos el niño que aparece en primer plano. Con toda seguridad, los demás murieron en los campos de exterminio.

Ebrei civili del ghetto di Varsavia si arrendono ai soldati tedeschi nel 1943. Dei 600.000 ebrei che vi furono confinati solo 60.000 sopravvissero e, tra questi, anche il ragazzo in primo piano nella foto. La maggior parte perì nei campi di sterminio.

The battle for Stalingrad, 1943. Soviet troops defend the ruins of the Red October plant in some of the bitterest fighting of the war.

La batalla de Stalingrado, en 1943. Soldados soviéticos defienden las ruinas de la fábrica Octubre Rojo en uno de los enfrentamientos más terribles de la guerra.

La battaglia di Stalingrado, 1943. Soldati sovietici difendono le rovine della fabbrica Ottobre Rosso in uno degli scontri più sanguinosi di tutta la guerra.

The battle of Kursk, 1943. A German artilleryman sits on the remains of his gun, a dead comrade by his side.

La batalla de Kursk, en 1943. Un soldado de artillería alemán, sentado sobre los restos de su cañón. A su lado yace muerto uno de sus camaradas.

La battaglia di Kursk, 1943. Un artigliere tedesco siede su ciò che resta del suo cannone, un camerata giace morto accanto a lui.

The last few minutes before 'hitting the beach'. American soldiers shelter in their landing craft early in the war. It was a scene repeated a thousand times all over the world, from Europe to North Africa to the Pacific Islands.

Los últimos minutos antes de alcanzar la playa. Soldados estadounidenses escondidos dentro de una barcaza, al principio de la guerra. Fue una escena repetida miles de veces en todo el mundo, desde Europa hasta el norte de África y las islas del Pacífico.

Gli ultimi minuti prima di raggiungere la spiaggia. Soldati americani si riparano nei loro mezzi di sbarco all'inizio della guerra. Scene come questa dovevano ripetersi migliaia di volte in tutto il mondo: dall'Europa all'Africa del Nord alle isole del Pacifico.

The soft underbelly of the Nazi empire. Allied troops commanded by General Patton wade ashore during the invasion of Sicily in July 1943. Eisenhower called it 'the first page in the liberation of the European continent'.

El talón de Aquiles de los nazis. Desembarco de tropas aliadas al mando del general Patton durante la invasión de Sicilia, en julio de 1943. Eisenhower lo denominó "la primera página en la liberación del continente europeo".

Il tallone d'Achille nazista. Truppe alleate guidate dal generale Patton raggiungono la spiaggia durante lo sbarco in Sicilia nel luglio del 1943. Eisenhower lo definirà "Il primo passo verso la liberazione del continente europeo".

Striking inland. Just a couple of miles from Utah
Beach in Normandy, American soldiers of the US 4th
Army rain shells on retreating German soldiers in
the little town of Carentan. Great battles lay ahead.

Ataques en el frente. A sólo unos kilómetros
de la playa de Utah, en Normandía, soldados
estadounidenses del 4.º Ejército hacen llover bombas
sobre los soldados alemanes en retirada en la
pequeña ciudad de Carentan. Aún quedaban grandes
batallas por librar.

Attacco dietro la linea del fronte. A qualche
chilometro da Utah Beach, in Normandia, soldati
della IV armata americana fanno piovere bombe sui
soldati tedeschi che si ritirano verso la piccola città
di Carentan. Ma le grandi battaglie devono ancora
arrivare.

Russian infantrymen fight their way street by street through the suburbs of Berlin, May 1945. The Reich was in its death throes.

Soldados de infantería rusos se abren paso calle a calle en las afueras de Berlín, en mayo de 1945. El Reich estaba agonizando.

Fanti russi combattono strada per strada alla periferia di Berlino, maggio 1945. Il Reich è ormai in agonia.

November 1944.
US Army Captain
Tom Carothers and
Lieutenant Roy
Green display the
'liberated' jacket of a
German general.

Noviembre de 1944.
El capitán Tom
Carothers y el
lugarteniente Roy
Green del ejército
estadounidense
muestran la
chaqueta "liberada"
de un general
alemán.

Novembre 1944.
Il capitano d'armata
americano Tom
Carothers e il
luogotenente Roy
Green mostrano la
giacca "liberata" di
un generale tedesco.

The aftermath of war. Cologne Cathedral stands above the ruins of a great
city. In the foreground is the twisted metal of the Hohenzollernbrücke. The
picture was taken in 1946, a year after the war ended.

Las secuelas de la guerra. La catedral de Colonia se alza sobre las ruinas de una
gran ciudad. En primer plano, los hierros doblegados del puente Hohenzollern.
La foto se tomó en 1946, un año después de que finalizara la guerra.

Le conseguentze della guerra. La cattedrale di Colonia si staglia sulle rovine
della città. In primo piano è il ponte Hohenzollern distrutto. La foto è stata
scattata nel 1946, un anno dopo la fine della guerra.

British, Russian and American troops on the balcony of the Chancellery in Berlin celebrate the death of Hitler.

Soldados británicos, rusos y estadounidenses en el balcón de la Cancillería, en Berlín, celebran la muerte de Hitler.

Soldati britannici, russi e americani al balcone della Cancelleria del Reich a Berlino, celebrano la morte di Hitler.

April 1944. US troops on the Pacific island of Bougainville prepare for a reconnaissance mission. As the Americans advanced through the North Solomon Islands, they frequently left behind them Japanese pockets of resistance that had to be cleared by following troops.

Abril de 1944. Soldados estadounidenses en la isla de Bougainville, en el Pacífico, se preparan para una misión de reconocimiento. Durante su avance por el norte de las islas Solomón, a menudo quedaban grupos de resistencia japoneses aislados, que las tropas que les seguían se encargaban de eliminar.

Aprile 1944. Truppe americane sull'isola di Bougainville, nel Pacifico, si preparano per una missione di ricognizione. A mano a mano che avanzavano verso il Nord delle isole Solomon, gli americani si lasciavano alle spalle sacche di resistenza giapponese che sarebbero state poi eliminate dalle truppe che seguivano.

A good year for the General. President Roosevelt (right) and Douglas MacArthur (far left) celebrate MacArthur's appointment as Chief of Staff of the US Army, 1944. In that year, MacArthur led the advance through the Pacific Islands, returned to the Philippines and was promoted to five-star general.

Un buen año para el general. El presidente Roosevelt (derecha) y Douglas MacArthur (extremo izquierdo) celebran el nombramiento de éste como jefe del estado mayor del ejército estadounidense, en 1944. Ese año, MacArthur dirigió el avance a través de las islas del Pacífico, volvió a las Filipinas y fue ascendido a general de cinco estrellas.

Un buon anno per il generale. Il presidente Roosevelt (a destra) e il generale Douglas MacArthur (all'estrema sinistra) celebrano la promozione di MacArthur a capo di stato maggiore dell'esercito americano, nel 1944. In quell'anno MacArthur guiderà l'offensiva nelle isole del Pacifico. Tornato dalle Filippine sarà promosso generale a cinque stelle.

Two minds with but a single thought: 'Who gets the bigger influence over Europe when the fighting stops?' Allied leaders Stalin and Churchill in a rare moment of joviality at the Yalta (Ukraine) Conference in February 1945.

Dos mentes pero una sola idea: "¿Quién conseguirá tener mayor influencia en Europa cuando termine la guerra?" Los líderes aliados Stalin y Churchill en uno de los escasos momentos de distensión durante la Conferencia de Yalta (Ucrania), en febrero de 1945.

Due spiriti ma un solo pensiero: "Chi eserciterà maggiore influenza sull'Europa alla fine della guerra?" I leader alleati Stalin e Churchill in un raro momento di rilassamento alla conferenza di Yalta, in Ucraina, nel febbraio 1945.

Defeat for Germany. General Alfred Jodl (centre) signs the German surrender at Allied commander Eisenhower's headquarters in Reims on 7 May 1945. On the left is Major Wilhelm Orenius, on the right Admiral of the Fleet Georg von Friedeburg.

La capitulación de Alemania. El general Alfred Jodl (centro) firma la rendición alemana en los cuarteles generales aliados del comandante Eisenhower, en Reims, el 7 de mayo de 1945. A la izquierda se encuentra el mayor Wilhelm Orenius, y a la derecha, el almirante de la flota Georg von Friedeburg.

La sconfitta della Germania. Il generale Alfred Jodl (al centro) firma la resa tedesca al quartier generale alleato di Eisenhower, Reims, 7 maggio 1945. A sinistra il maggiore Wilhelm Orenius, a destra l'ammiraglio della flotta Georg von Friedeburg.

Defeat for Japan. The Japanese Foreign Minister, Mamoro Shigemitsu, discusses surrender terms with Lieutenant General Richard Sutherland on board the USS *Missouri*.

La capitulación de Japón. El ministro de Asuntos Exteriores de Japón, Mamoro Shigemitsu, discute los términos de la rendición con el general lugarteniente Richard Sutherland, a bordo del USS *Missouri*.

La sconfitta del Giappone. Il ministro giapponese degli Affari esteri, Mamoro Shigemitsu, discute i termini della resa con il luogotenente generale Richard Sutherland a bordo della USS *Missouri*.

2. The home front
El frente en casa
Il fronte interno

'London can take it.' At the height of the Blitz, a London family emerges from the ruins of their house with the prized possessions that they have salvaged, including grandma's potted plant.

"Londres puede conseguirlo". En el apogeo del *Blitz,* los ataques aéreos sobre la capital británica, una familia londinense emerge de entre las ruinas de su casa con algunas de las posesiones que han podido salvar, incluida la planta de la abuela.

"Londra ce la può fare". All'apice del Blitz (il bombardamento della città) una famiglia londinese emerge dalle rovine della propria casa mostrando fieramente quello che sono riusciti a salvare, compresa la pianta della nonna.

2. The home front
El frente en casa
Il fronte interno

It was the citizens' war. Heinkels, Halifaxes and Flying Fortresses brought the horrors of war to suburban streets and city centres. No one was safe. The shelter in the back garden or the platform of a tube station were constant reminders that everyone was involved in the fighting.

There were ration books and queues for food. When a few extra onions were available, word spread quickly, and butchers and greengrocers had a hard time convincing all of their even-handedness. There was the blackout: a mere chink of light brought the fury of an air raid warden down upon a house – but that was better than a bomb.

Children were sent away from the cities to the comparative safety of the country. Some enjoyed the change. Some hated it. A few walked doggedly back home. It depended on the child and the sort of welcome they received.

Old men and boys dressed in uniforms and guarded crossroads, coastlines, railway tunnels. Everyone was told to guard their tongues: 'Careless talk costs lives;' 'Be like Dad, keep Mum.'

Somehow civilization survived. And before the 1940s were over, there were even some who looked back on the war years with a fond nostalgia.

La Segunda Guerra Mundial fue una guerra contra la población civil. Los Heinkel, los Halifax y las fortalezas volantes trajeron los horrores de la guerra a las calles de pueblos y ciudades. Nadie estaba seguro. El refugio construido en el jardín trasero o el andén de una estación de metro recordaban a cada momento que todo el mundo estaba implicado en la lucha.

Había cartillas de racionamiento y colas para obtener alimentos. Si en alguna ocasión una tienda disponía de algún producto en abundancia, la noticia corría veloz y los comerciantes tenían que apresurarse a defender su inocencia. Por la noche debían apagarse todas las luces.

Al menor rayo de luz que saliese de una casa, los vigilantes de ataques aéreos acudían enfurecidos, lo que sin duda era preferible a morir víctimas de una bomba.

Los más pequeños fueron evacuados al campo, que era relativamente más seguro que la ciudad. A algunos el cambio de vida les gustó, pero otros no consiguieron adaptarse e incluso regresaron a casa a pie. Todo dependía de las características de cada niño o niña y de la bienvenida que recibiesen lejos del hogar.

Los ancianos y los chicos más jóvenes se pusieron uniformes y se encargaron de vigilar los cruces de carreteras, las playas y los túneles de ferrocarril. Todos recibieron la consigna de contener la lengua: "Hablar demasiado cuesta vidas humanas".

De una forma u otra, la civilización logró sobrevivir. Antes de que terminara la década, algunos incluso sintieron cierta nostalgia al pensar en los años de guerra.

Fu la guerra dei civili. Heinkel, Halifax, fortezze volanti portarono l'orrore nelle periferie e nel centro delle città. Nessuno aveva scampo. I rifugi nel giardino di casa o nelle banchine delle metropolitane erano un monito costante: ognuno era coinvolto nella guerra.

Comparvero le tessere del razionamento e le code per il cibo. Quando arrivava qualche cipolla in più la voce si spargeva immediatamente e macellai e ortolani avevano un bel da fare per convincere i clienti della loro imparzialità. Poi il coprifuoco: il più piccolo raggio di luce poteva scatenare le furie delle guardie contro i raid: meglio comunque che subire l'esplosione di una bomba.

I bambini furono mandati lontano dalle città, nelle relativamente più sicure campagne. Alcuni apprezzarono questo cambiamento, altri lo odiarono. Alcuni tornarono a casa a piedi come dei cani. Dipendeva dal carattere dei bambini e da come erano accolti.

Vecchi e bambini portavano l'uniforme e sorvegliavano gli incroci, le coste, le gallerie ferroviarie. A tutti era raccomandato di tenere la lingua a posto: "L'imprudenza costa vite umane", "Fai come papà, proteggi la mamma".

Qualche forma di civiltà comunque sopravvisse. E prima che gli anni Quaranta finissero c'era chi ricordava gli anni di guerra con una punta di nostalgia.

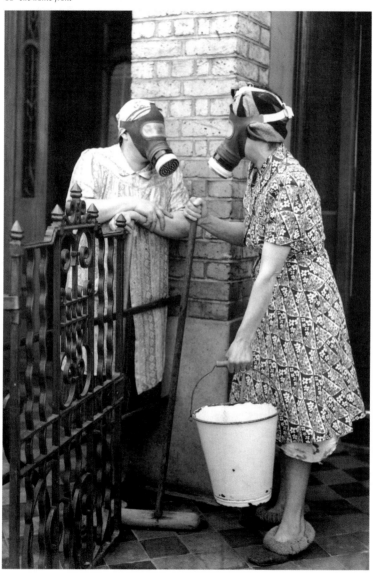

Though they were seldom needed in earnest, even on the Home Front everyone had to get used to wearing their gas mask.

Aunque es cierto que muy pocas veces tuvieron que utilizarse, incluso en el "frente del interior" todo el mundo debía acostumbrarse a llevar su máscara de gas.

Anche se in realtà furono usate molto raramente, anche nel fronte interno ognuno dovette abituarsi a portare le maschere antigas.

Two steelworkers enjoy a cigarette during a break from work, November 1942. In peacetime, few women would have found work in such a place.

Dos obreras de una planta siderúrgica disfrutan de un cigarrillo durante un descanso, en noviembre de 1942. En tiempo de paz, pocas mujeres habrían encontrado trabajo en una fábrica de este tipo.

Due operaie di una acciaieria si gustano una sigaretta durante una pausa, novembre 1942. In tempo di pace è poco probabile che delle donne avrebbero trovato lavoro in una fabbrica di questo tipo.

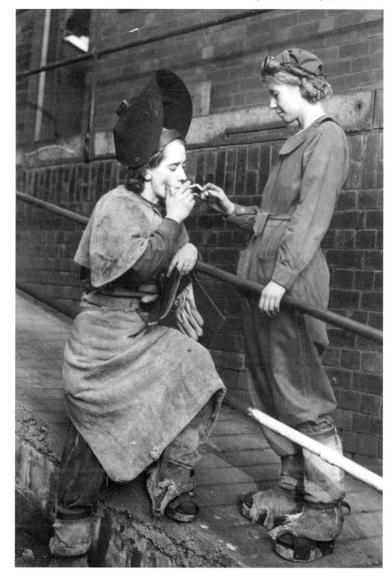

February 1941. Students work on a giant poster during Canterbury's
'Weapons Week'. 'Give us the tools' had become instantly famous as a
slogan, although Churchill had coined the phrase only 12 days earlier.

Febrero de 1941. Estudiantes trabajando en un póster gigante durante
la "Semana de las armas", en Canterbury. "Dadnos las herramientas"
se convirtió rápidamente en un famoso lema, acuñado por Churchill
tan sólo doce días antes.

Febbraio 1941. Alcuni studenti lavorano a un gigantesco manifesto
per la "Settimana delle armi" a Canterbury. "Dateci gli strumenti"
divenne immediatamente uno slogan molto popolare che Churchill
aveva coniato solo 12 giorni prima.

August 1940.
Hitler's last appeal
was dropped
from the skies.
Three weeks later
the Blitz began.

Agosto de 1940. El
último llamamiento
a la razón enviado
por Hitler a los
británicos fue
lanzado desde el
cielo. Tres semanas
más tarde empezaba
el *Blitz*, los ataques
aéreos sobre la
capital británica.

Agosto 1940.
L'ultimo "appello
alla ragione" di
Hitler fu lanciato
dai cieli. Tre
settimane più tardi
ebbe inizio il Blitz
(i bombardamenti
su Londra).

Dad's Army,
November 1942.
A member of the
25th Battalion
London Home
Guard demonstrates
the use of
camouflage.

El ejército de papá,
en noviembre de
1942. Un miembro
del 25.º batallón de
la fuerza de reserva
londinense hace una
demostración de
camuflaje.

L'esercito di papà,
novembre 1942.
Un membro del
XXV battaglione
territoriale londinese
a una dimostrazione
di mimetizzazione.

After being the bogyman of Europe for decades, the Soviet Union suddenly became an heroic ally in 1941. A Red Cross representative collects money for the Russian war effort in the Strand, London on an 'Aid to Russia' flag day.

Después de haber sido el temor de Europa durante décadas, la Unión Soviética se convirtió de pronto en un heroico aliado en 1941. Una colaboradora de la Cruz Roja recolecta dinero para apoyar el esfuerzo de guerra ruso, en el Strand (Londres), durante jornada "Ayuda a Rusia".

Dopo essere stato per decenni lo spauracchio d'Europa, l'Unione Sovietica divenne improvvisamente un alleato eroico. Una rappresentante della Croce rossa raccoglie nello Strand, a Londra, denaro per sostenere gli sforzi di guerra russi durante la giornata "Aiutate la Russia".

A huge campaign was mounted to save waste and recycle
materials. It was partly a morale-boosting exercise, to persuade
civilians that they could take an active part in the war. In this
case, the message was directed at the citizens of Cheltenham.

Para reducir la cantidad de deshechos y reciclar materiales, se
organizó una campaña a gran escala. En parte fue una estrategia
para subir la moral de la población civil y persuadirles de que
podían participar activamente en la guerra. En este caso, el
mensaje iba dirigido a los habitantes de Cheltenham.

Fu organizzata un'enorme campagna di recupero dei rifiuti e
di materiale riciclabile. Essa nacque anche dall'esigenza di
sostenere il morale delle popolazioni civili che si persuadevano
così di prendere parte attiva alla guerra. In questa foto il
messaggio è rivolto ai cittadini di Celtenham, in Inghilterra.

Southgate, London, 1942. To prevent pedestrians colliding in the blackout, these slogans were stencilled on pavements all over the city.

Southgate, Londres, en 1942. Para evitar que los transeúntes chocaran en la oscuridad durante los apagones, se pintaron las instrucciones adecuadas por toda la ciudad: "Circule por la izquierda".

Southgate, Londra, 1942. Per impedire collisioni tra i pedoni durante il coprifuoco queste scritte furono collocate in tutti i marciapiedi della città: "Camminare alla sinistra del marciapiede".

Rogue gift.
A volunteer holds a
German helmet,
mistakenly included
in a collection of
aluminium at the
Chelsea Town Hall,
July 1940.

Sentido del humor.
Una voluntaria
sostiene un casco
alemán enviado, tal
vez por error, a un
centro de recogida
de objetos de
aluminio en el
ayuntamiento
de Chelsea, en julio
de 1940.

Senso dell'umorismo.
Un'ausiliaria guarda
un elmetto tedesco
finito erroneamente
in una raccolta di
alluminio organizzata
dal municipio di
Chelsea, luglio 1940.

Wrought-iron railings are removed from Battersea Park, London, 1940. The Government claimed they were melted down to provide metal for weapons. Later, the poor pointed out that similar gates and railings from the houses of the rich had been left alone.

Verjas de hierro forjado retiradas de Battersea Park, Londres, en 1940. El gobierno pretendía fundirlas y obtener metal para fabricar armas. Más tarde dos pobres protestaron porque las verjas y puertas de las casas de los ricos habían quedado intactas.

Si smontano le inferriate del Battersea Park a Londra, 1940. Il governo britannico dichiarò che il metallo sarebbe stato fuso per la costruzione di armi. Successivamente però i poveri di Londra fecero notare che le inferriate che ornavano le case dei ricchi erano state risparmiate.

Preparing for the Blitz, July 1940. Workers demonstrate the use of bomb 'snuffers' to extinguish incendiary bombs.

Medidas preventivas contra el *Blitz*, los ataques aéreos contra Londres, en julio de 1940. Unos obreros muestran cómo utilizar "apagadores" para extinguir bombas incendiarias.

Ci si prepara al Blitz (i bombardamenti di Londra), luglio 1940. Operai mostrano il funzionamento di "estintori" per le bombe incendiarie.

The wife of the inventor of the 'bomb grab' shows how your front parlour can be saved in seconds.

La esposa del inventor del "recogebombas" demuestra cómo el salón de casa puede ponerse a salvo en cuestión de segundos.

La moglie dell'inventore del "catturabombe" dimostra come si può salvare un salotto in pochi secondi.

Mrs Whitham, mother of 16 children, tots up the 'points' in her family's ration books. The end of the war did not bring an end to rationing.

Mrs Whitham, madre de 16 hijos, anota "puntos" en las cartillas de racionamiento familiares. Desafortunadamente, el final de la guerra no supuso el fin del racionamiento.

Mrs Whitham, madre di 16 figli segna i "punti" nelle tessere del razionamento di famiglia. La fine della guerra però non sempre significò anche la fine del razionamento.

A shopkeeper tries to reassure customers. This picture was taken in February 1940. Within a short while many more items 'went on ration'.

Un comerciante intenta atraer clientes con un cartel que informa de que sólo tres de sus productos están racionados. La foto es de febrero de 1940. Poco después se racionarían muchos más artículos.

Un salumiere cerca di rassicurare i clienti. La foto fu scattata nel febbraio dell 1940. Poco tempo dopo molti altri prodotti furono razionati.

'If you want to get ahead…' British troops fought in a vast variety of climates for king and country. Here a consignment of pith helmets, probably for India, receives a quality inspection before they are dispatched, August 1942.

"Para no perder la cabeza..." Los soldados británicos lucharon por el rey y la patria en regiones con climas muy diversos. En la foto, una partida de cascos coloniales, probablemente con destino a la India, pasa una inspección antes de ser enviada, en agosto de 1942.

"Se vuoi avere successo…" I soldati britannici combattevano a tutte le latitudini immaginabili per il re e per la patria. Nella foto una consegna di elmetti, probabilmente destinati all'India, è oggetto di un controllo di qualità prima della spedizione, agosto 1942.

'... get a hat.'
Women workers in a
factory add the final
touches to khaki
tam-o'-shanters for a
Scottish regiment,
September 1940.

"... ponte un
sombrero". Obreras
de una fábrica dan
los toques finales a
las boinas caqui
destinadas a un
regimiento escocés,
en septiembre de
1940.

"... comprati un
cappello". Operaie
di una fabbrica
danno l'ultimo tocco
ai berretti color
cachi destinati a un
reggimento scozzese,
settembre 1940.

The Government struggled to reassure people at home that they could be protected from air raids. Herbert Morrison, Minister of Home Security, introduced the new indoor table shelter to the House of Commons in 1941.

El gobierno se esforzó por convencer a la población de que en casa podían estar a salvo de los ataques aéreos. Herbert Morrison, ministro de Seguridad Interior, presentó al Parlamento esta singular mesa-refugio en 1941.

Il governo faceva ogni sforzo per convincere la popolazione che ci si poteva proteggere dai bombardamenti aerei. Herbert Morrison, ministro della sicurezza interna, presentò al Parlamento questo tavolo-rifugio da salotto nel 1941.

Family model. Wembley Council provided this indoor shelter made of timber and corrugated iron in January 1941.

Modelo familiar. En enero de 1941, el consejo municipal de Wembley proporcionó a los ciudadanos este refugio de madera y chapa de zinc para el interior de las viviendas.

Modello familiare. Il consiglio municipale di Wembley presenta ai cittadini questo rifugio per casa in legno e ferro ondulato, gennaio 1941.

Some shelters were built for only one. This structure was supplied as a refuge for the guardsman on duty outside Marlborough House, London in 1940. He may well have had to remove his busby to fit in it.

Algunos refugios tenían una sola plaza. La estructura de la foto es el refugio de los guardas de Marlborough House, en Londres, en 1940. Sin duda tenían que quitarse el gorro militar para entrar en él.

Alcuni rifugi furono progettati per una sola persona. Questo modello doveva proteggere una sentinella in servizio a Malborough House a Londra nel 1941. Con ogni probabilità però avrebbe dovuto togliere il copricapo per poterlo utilizzare.

Special protection for a Very Important Person. This is the 'Churchill Egg', a pressurized cabin designed for the prime minister's private use when flying at a high altitude. If the great man smoked his cigars inside, it's a wonder he didn't asphyxiate himself.

Un refugio especial para un VIP. Este es el "Huevo de Churchill", una cabina presurizada para los viajes a gran altitud que realizaba el primer ministro. Si seguía fumando sus enormes puros en el interior, es sorprendente que no se asfixiara.

Protezione speciale per un VIP. L'"uovo di Churchill", una cabina pressurizzata per uso privato del primo ministro durante i voli a grande altezza. Se però il grand'uomo vi avesse fumato il sigaro all'interno non sarebbe sopravvissuto all'asfissia.

For houses without gardens, chains of street shelters were supplied. In 1941 there was no parking problem in a London street like this.

Para las casas sin jardín se colocaron refugios en las calles. En 1941 no había problemas de aparcamiento en las calles de Londres.

Per le case senza giardino furono fabbricati rifugi come questi. Nel 1941 non c'erano problemi di parcheggio nelle strade di Londra.

A typical scene in a tube station during the Blitz. Londoners spend the night on a stationary escalator.

Un escena típica en una estación de metro durante el *Blitz,* los ataques aéreos sobre Londres. Una escalera mecánica detenida servía de cama para muchos londinenses.

Tipica scena in una stazione della metropolitana durante il Blitz (i bombardamenti su Londra). Londinesi passano la notte in una scala mobile ferma.

Councils were organized to run the London Underground shelters. Families had regular pitches. The platform was more comfortable than the stairs.

Se organizaron comités para gestionar los refugios del metro de Londres. Algunas familias tenían asignado un lugar determinado. Sin duda los andenes eran más cómodos que las escaleras.

Furono organizzati dei comitati per gestire i rifugi della metropolitana di Londra. Le famiglie avevano dei posti regolari. La banchina era più comoda delle scale mobili.

Muscovites shelter in the Maiakovskaia Underground station during the German bombardment in 1941. The stations were also used as hospitals.

Moscovitas refugiados en la estación de metro de Maiakovskaia durante los bombardeos alemanes de 1941. Las estaciones también se utilizaban como hospitales.

Moscoviti si rifugiano nella stazione della metropolitana Maiakovskaia durante i bombardamenti tedeschi del 1941. La stazione fu usata anche come ospedale.

Evacuated treasures. A Goliath frog from the Natural History Museum finds a wartime home in Surrey caves, March 1943.

Tesoros evacuados. Durante la guerra, esta rana gigante del museo de historia natural del Reino Unido encontró refugio en las cuevas de Surrey, en marzo de 1943.

Tesori evacuati. Una rana gigante del Museo di storia naturale trova rifugio in una cantina del Surrey nel marzo 1943.

Sir Kenneth Clark, Director of the National Gallery, checks the well-being of some of the nation's masterpieces in their North Wales hideaway, 1942. The Gallery was emptied of its greatest paintings, but itself escaped damage.

Sir Kenneth Clark, director de la National Gallery de Londres, comprueba el buen estado de algunas de las obras maestras británicas, escondidas en algún lugar del norte de Gales, en 1942. Se trasladaron los principales cuadros de la National Gallery, que afortunadamente no sufrieron ningún daño.

Sir Kenneth Clark, direttore della National Gallery, verifica il buono stato di alcuni capolavori nel loro rifugio nel Galles settentrionale, 1942. Svuotato dei dipinti più importanti, il museo comunque non subì alcun danno.

The ruins of the old St Thomas's Hospital, London after an enemy raid.
The hospital was heavily bombed and had to be completely rebuilt after
the war. The Palace of Westminster also suffered, but not so disastrously.

Las ruinas del viejo hospital de St Thomas, en Londres, tras un ataque
aéreo enemigo. El hospital, intensamente bombardeado, tuvo que
reconstruirse completamente después de la guerra. El Palacio de
Westminster también sufrió daños, pero de menor importancia.

Le rovine del vecchio ospedale di St Thomas a Londra dopo un
bombardamento. Gravemente danneggiato, l'ospedale fu completamente
ricostruito dopo la guerra. Anche il palazzo di Westminster fu colpito ma
non altrettanto gravemente.

Soldiers clear the rubble from the Bank Underground station. Like St Paul's Cathedral, the Mansion House (in the background) sustained only slight damage.

Unos soldados retiran los escombros de la estación de metro Bank. Al igual que la catedral de St Paul, la Mansion House (al fondo) no sufrió daños graves.

Soldati ripuliscono le rovine davanti alla stazione Bank della metropolitana. Come la cattedrale di St Paul anche la Mansion House (sullo sfondo) non subì seri danni.

Balham High Street,
October 1940.
A witness of the
Blitz wrote, 'The
earth seemed to
split into a thousand
fragments.'

Balham High Street,
en octubre de 1940.
Un testimonio de los
bombardeos del *Blitz*
escribió: "Pareció
que el suelo se partía
en mil pedazos".

Balham High Street,
ottobre 1940.
Un testimone del
bombardamento
scrisse: "La terra
sembrava spaccarsi
in migliaia di
frammenti".

Canterbury, June 1942. A newly homeless family sets out to find somewhere to live.

Canterbury, junio de 1942. Una familia que acaba de perder su casa busca un lugar para instalarse.

Canterbury, giugno 1942. Una famiglia che ha perso la casa alla ricerca di un posto dove vivere.

Wedding Day, 1940. It became a matter of pride on all home fronts that everything in life and business should carry on as usual. The marriage rate actually increased. Men and women saw getting married during the war as an act of faith.

El día de la boda, en 1940. Lograr que la vida continuara con normalidad se convirtió en una cuestión de dignidad para todos los ciudadanos. De hecho, el número de matrimonios aumentó. Hombres y mujeres consideraban que casarse durante la guerra era un acto de fe.

Nozze nel 1940. Era motivo di orgoglio, nel fronte interno, che ogni cosa continuasse a funzionare come al solito. Il numero dei matrimoni infatti crebbe. Per uomini e donne sposarsi in tempo di guerra divenne un atto di fede.

London, October 1940. While firemen damp down the smouldering ruins behind him,
a milkman picks his way through rubble to deliver the morning's supply. Churchill's words
to Hitler voiced the feelings of many Londoners: 'You do your worst – and we will do our best.'

Londres, octubre de 1940. Mientras los bomberos terminan su trabajo entre ruinas humeantes,
un lechero se abre paso entre los escombros para realizar su reparto diario. Las palabras que
Churchill dirigió a Hitler reflejan el sentimiento de muchos londinenses: "Vosotros hacéis lo
peor que podéis. Nosotros lo haremos lo mejor que podamos".

Londra, ottobre 1940. Mentre i pompieri spengono il fuoco tra le rovine fumanti alle sue
spalle, un lattaio si fa strada per le sue consegne del mattino. Le parole di Churchill a Hitler
risuonavano nelle orecchie di molti londinesi: "Voi fate il peggio; noi faremo del nostro
meglio".

Old Kent Road, London, September 1940. Business as usual for a postman collecting mail from a battered pillar box.

Old Kent Road (Londres), en septiembre de 1940. Entre los escombros, un cartero recoge el correo de un buzón como de costumbre.

Old Kent Road, settembre 1940. Come ogni giorno un postino raccoglie la posta da una buca delle lettere bombardata.

Dressed more for the camera than her surroundings, artist Ethel Gabain paints a scene
of air raid damage for the Ministry of Information, November 1940. The Government
believed that paintings often served better than photographs as propaganda.

La artista Ethel Gabain, vestida más para la cámara que para el escenario de ruinas,
pinta los daños producidos por los ataques aéreos para el ministerio de Información,
en noviembre de 1940. El gobierno creía que a menudo los cuadros eran más útiles
como propaganda que las fotografías.

Ben vestita per il fotografo e ben piazzata nella desolazione delle rovine, l'artista Ethel
Gabain dipinge una scena di bombardamento per il ministero dell'informazione,
novembre 1940. Il governo era convinto che, per la propaganda, spesso i dipinti
fossero più efficaci delle fotografie.

'Business as usual' at its most absurd. Readers browse among the charred remains of the Earl of Ilchester's library at Holland House in 1941. The house was so badly damaged that it was left derelict until 1952.

"La vida continúa" en sus formas más absurdas. Unos lectores consultan libros entre los restos calcinados de la biblioteca del conde de Ilchester, en Holland House, en 1941. Este edificio quedó tan gravemente dañado que no se reconstruyó hasta 1952.

" La vita continua" anche nei frangenti più assurdi. Lettori guardano tra gli scaffali della biblioteca devastata del conte di Ilchester a Holland House, 1941. L'edificio fu così pesantemente danneggiato da poter essere ricostruito soltanto nel 1952.

The men who captured the news – good or bad. Fred
Ramage at work during the foggy days of 1946. Several
of the photographs in chapter 5 were taken by him.

El hombre que capturaba las noticias, fuesen buenas o
malas, a través de su objetivo. Fred Ramage en pleno
trabajo un día de niebla de 1946. Varias de las
fotografías del capítulo 5 de este libro son suyas.

L'uomo che cattura le notizie – buone o cattive. Fred
Ramage al lavoro durante una nebbiosa giornata del
1946. Molte delle fotografie del capitolo 5 furono
scattate da lui.

Reporters dash to the phones to file their copy after hearing sentences passed on Nazi war criminals at the Palace of Justice, Nuremberg, in 1946. The trials began in November 1945 and lasted until 1947.

Varios reporteros se precipitan hacia los teléfonos para transmitir en sus crónicas las sentencias contra los criminales de guerra nazis pronunciadas en el Palacio de Justicia de Núremberg, en 1946. Los juicios empezaron en noviembre de 1945 y duraron hasta 1947.

I giornalisti si precipitano ai telefoni per trasmettere gli articoli dopo avere sentito le sentenze contro i criminali di guerra al palazzo di giustizia di Norimberga, nel 1946. Il processo era cominciato nel 1945 e terminerà nel 1947.

The last desperate gamble. In 1944 the Nazis began their V1 and
V2 flying bomb raids on London and the Home Counties.
Here a man is rescued from the wreckage of his London home.

El último gesto desesperado. En 1944 los nazis iniciaron sus
ataques aéreos con los proyectiles V1 y V2 sobre Londres y los
condados cercanos. En la foto, un londinense rescatado de entre
las ruinas de su casa.

L'ultimo disperato tentativo. Nel 1944 i nazisti cominciano il
lancio delle bombe volanti V1 e V2 contro Londra e le aree
circostanti. Nella foto un uomo soccorso dopo la distruzione
della sua casa.

This V2 rocket attack killed 300 civilians in Farringdon Market, London, March 1945.

El ataque con proyectiles V2 sobre el mercado de Farringdon, Londres, en marzo de 1945, ocasionó 300 muertes entre la población civil.

Questo attacco con bombe V2 provocò la morte di 300 civili a Farringdon, Londra 1945.

The cost of liberation,
December 1944. A Dutch
boy stands in front of the
wreckage of his home.

El precio de la liberación,
diciembre de 1944. Un
joven holandés delante de
su casa destruida.

Il prezzo della liberazione,
dicembre 1944. Un
giovane olandese davanti
a ciò che resta della sua
casa.

The cost of defeat, July 1945. Berliners, with the few possessions they have left, in the ruins of the Nollendorfplatz.

El precio de la derrota, julio de 1945. Un grupo de berlineses, con las pocas pertenencias que han podido salvar, pasan ante las ruinas de la plaza Nollendorf.

Il prezzo della sconfitta, luglio 1945. Berlinesi con il poco che sono riusciti a salvare tra le rovine di Nollendorfplatz.

And all for £3 a week. A fireman tackles a blaze 80 feet (25 metres) above a London street, February 1941.

Y todo por tan sólo tres libras esterlinas a la semana. Un bombero extingue un incendio a 25 metros de altura en una calle de Londres, en febrero de 1941.

E tutto questo per 3 sterline alla settimana. Un pompiere spegne un incendio a 25 metri d'altezza in una strada di Londra, febbraio 1941.

Local civilian women firefighters struggling to control the fires that raged in
Pearl Harbor after the Japanese attack, 7 December 1941. Twenty-two
warships were sunk or damaged, 200 planes destroyed, 2,400 people killed.

Bomberas voluntarias intentan controlar los incendios que arrasaron Pearl
Harbour tras el ataque japonés del 7 de diciembre de 1941, en el que
22 buques de guerra se hundieron o resultaron dañados, 200 aviones
quedaron destruidos y murieron 2.400 personas.

Donne civili del luogo combattono contro l'incendio divampato dopo
l'attacco aereo giapponese a Pearl Harbour il 7 dicembre 1941. Furono
uccise 2400 persone, 22 navi da guerra colarono a picco e 200 aerei furono
distrutti.

Undesirable aliens. American police search a bewildered group of
Japanese residents. The Japanese were seen as potential saboteurs by
the US authorities, even in the days before the attack on Pearl Harbor.

Extranjeros indeseables. La policía estadounidense registra a un grupo
de residentes japoneses desorientados. Las autoridades norteamericanas
consideraban a los japoneses saboteadores en potencia, incluso durante
los días que precedieron al ataque sobre Pearl Harbour.

Stranieri indesiderabili. La polizia americana controlla un gruppo di
disorientati emigrati giapponesi. I giapponesi erano visti come
potenziali sabotatori dalle autorità americane anche nel periodo
precedente l'attacco a Pearl Harbor.

In Britain, people of Italian and German origin were rounded up and interned. A group of women aliens are escorted by police to a London station, on the way to camps on the Isle of Man.

En el Reino Unido, a las personas de origen italiano y alemán se les reunía e internaba. En la foto, agentes de policía conducen a un grupo de mujeres extranjeras hacia una estación de Londres, desde donde se les llevará a uno de los campos de internamiento de la isla de Man.

In Gran Bretagna le persone di origine italiana e tedesca furono rastrellate e internate. Un gruppo di donne straniere è scortata dalla polizia alla stazione di Londra. Raggiungeranno un campo di detenzione nell'isola di Man.

In 1941 the British Government took the unprecedented step of
conscripting women for war service. The main opponents of this step
were men, women in general accepted it. Here women born in 1919
register at a labour exchange.

En 1941 el gobierno británico tomó una medida sin precedentes: alistar a
mujeres para la guerra. Los hombres fueron los que más se opusieron a
esta medida, mientras que las mujeres, en general, la aceptaron. En la foto,
cinco mujeres nacidas en 1919 registrándose.

Nel 1941, il governo britannico prese la decisione storica di reclutare le
donne per i servizi di guerra. I maggiori oppositori a questa scelta erano
uomini, mentre le donne generalmente l'accettarono. Nella foto donne del
1919 si iscrivono a un ufficio del lavoro.

Members of the ATS service a six-wheel truck at an army depot. By 1944 over half a million British women were serving in the armed forces, and millions more had been drafted into the Land Army and factories.

Miembros del ATS (servicio territorial auxiliar) reparan un camión de seis ruedas en un depósito del ejército. En 1944, más de medio millón de británicas prestaban servicio en las fuerzas armadas y otros tantos millones habían sido reclutadas para el ejército de tierra y para trabajar en las fábricas.

Ausiliarie lavorano su un camion a sei ruote in un deposito militare. Nel 1944 circa mezzo milione di donne lavoravano nelle forze armate e milioni di loro erano state reclutate per lavorare nella riserva e nelle fabbriche.

Seaside danger.
An elderly woman
examines a mine
washed up on the
east coast of
England, April 1940.

Peligro en la playa.
Una mujer examina
una mina arrastrada
por el mar hasta
la costa este de
Inglaterra, en abril
de 1940.

Pericoli del mare.
Un'anziana donna
esamina una mina
arenata sulle coste
dell'Inghilterra
nell'aprile del 1940.

Country safety.
A mother and baby
prepare to leave
London, November
1940. The mother is
carrying a special gas
mask for babies.

La zona rural era
más segura que las
ciudades. Una
madre y su hijo
se disponen a
abandonar Londres,
en noviembre de
1940. La madre
lleva una máscara de
gas especial para
bebés.

Sicurezza in
campagna. Una
madre e il suo
bambino si
preparano a lasciare
Londra nel
novembre del 1940.
La madre ha una
speciale maschera
antigas per il figlio.

Mixing with the locals. A GI gains the undivided attention of a
waitress at Rainbow Corner, Piccadilly Circus, in January 1944. The
café was established as a venue for American service personnel.

Contacto con la población local. Un soldado del GI acapara la
atención de una camarera del Rainbow Corner, en Piccadilly Circus,
en enero de 1944. Este café era un lugar de encuentro de militares
estadounidenses.

Contatti con i locali. Un GI gode dell'attenzione esclusiva di una
cameriera del Rainbow Corner a Piccadilly Circus, gennaio 1944.
Questo caffè era un luogo d'incontro abituale per i militari
americani.

Safe return. A member of the British Expeditionary Force receives an ecstatic welcome from his girlfriend on his return from Dunkirk. 'Operation Dynamo' was, in Churchill's words, 'a miracle of deliverance'. Over 330,000 men were rescued.

De regreso sano y salvo. Un miembro del cuerpo expedicionario británico recibe la apasionada bienvenida de su novia a la vuelta de Dunquerque. En palabras del propio Churchill, la operación Dynamo fue "un milagro de liberación". Más de 330.000 hombres fueron rescatados.

A casa sano e salvo. Un membro del corpo di spedizione britannico riceve un appassionato bacio di benvenuto al suo ritorno da Dunkerque. L'"Operazione Dinamo" fu, nelle parole di Churchill, "un miracolo della liberazione". Furono salvati più di 330.000 uomini.

As the build-up of men and equipment for D-day reaches its height, US troops join in a children's game 'somewhere in the south of England'. Most people knew the invasion of Europe was imminent, but few guessed where it would take place.

Mientras la concentración de hombres y material para el día D va tocando a su fin, unos soldados estadounidenses juegan con un grupo de niños "en algún lugar del sur de Inglaterra". Casi todo el mundo sabía que la invasión de Europa era inminente, pero pocos adivinaron dónde se realizaría.

Mentre la concentrazione di uomini e materiali per il D-day giunge al culmine, i soldati americani giocano con dei bambini "da qualche parte nell'Inghilterra meridionale". La maggior parte della gente sapeva che l'invasione dell'Europa era imminente, ma pochi potevano immaginare dove avrebbe avuto luogo.

The Pheasantry Club, London, 1940. Pre-war night clubs survived and even prospered during the war. Whisky and champagne were occasionally in short supply, but the bands played on and there were always plenty of dance partners.

El Pheasantry Club de Londres, en 1940. Los clubes nocturnos de antes de la guerra sobrevivieron e incluso prosperaron durante la contienda. A veces el whisky y el champán se terminaban, pero las orquestas seguían tocando y no era difícil encontrar pareja de baile.

Il Pheasantry Club, Londra 1940. I night club sopravvissero e anzi prosperarono durante la guerra. Whisky e champagne scarseggiavano, ma le orchestre suonavano e c'era sempre disponibilità di accompagnatori con cui ballare.

Night clubs were prohibitively expensive for the masses. They flocked instead to the local dance halls, where the bands were as good, the floor as packed, and the opportunities for romance every bit as enticing.

Los clubes nocturnos eran demasiado caros para la mayoría de las personas, que preferían reunirse en grandes salas de baile, donde las orquestas eran igual de buenas, la pista estaba igual de llena y las posibilidades de conocer a alguien eran si cabe mayores.

I night club erano troppo cari per la maggioranza delle persone. Si preferiva incontrarsi in enormi sale da ballo dove le orchestre erano altrettanto buone, il pavimento altrettanto cerato e le opportunità di rimorchiare non mancavano certamente.

3. Tools and training
Herramientas y formación
Strumenti e formazione

Sailors of the British Navy prepare to drop their cargo of
mines, 1940. In the early part of the war German U-boats,
operating from French ports, had the upper hand in the
war at sea. At the height of the Battle of the Atlantic up to
700,000 tons of shipping were sunk in a single month.

Marineros de la armada británica se preparan para lanzar
minas, en 1940. Al principio de la contienda, los
submarinos alemanes que operaban desde puertos
franceses dominaban la guerra en alta mar. En el punto
álgido de la Batalla del Atlántico llegaron a hundir hasta
700.000 toneladas de embarcaciones en un solo mes.

Marinai della British Navy si preparano a sganciare il loro
carico di mine, 1940. All'inizio della guerra i sottomarini
tedeschi, che operavano dai porti francesi, avevano il
predominio nella guerra sui mari. Al culmine della
battaglia dell'Atlantico in un solo mese colarono a picco
navi per un peso complessivo di 700.000 tonnellate.

3. Tools and training
   Herramientas y formación
   Strumenti e formazione

With the exception of the Pacific theatre, World War II was fought in the northern hemisphere in what is today called the 'developed world'. Here whole economies were turned over to war production. The entire populations and all the resources of Italy, France, Germany, Britain, the Soviet Union and the United States were devoted to supplying the guns or firing them.

Politicians and generals alike screamed for more planes, ships, tanks. At times of crisis, quantity control was more important than quality control. With millions of men engaged in combat, women now played a key role in keeping the weapons coming.

There was work to be done that people had never dreamed of doing: fire-fighting, plane-spotting, billeting children and displaced persons, running tea and coffee stalls for returning troops. Women who had been in domestic service suddenly found themselves aiming anti-aircraft guns, men who had worked in 'gentlemen's outfitting' learnt how to kill.

When the war was all over, and the swords were turned back into ploughshares, millions had to be retrained, factories had to be re-tooled. As for the women who had worked in farms and factories, most went back to being housewives.

Con la excepción del escenario del Pacífico, la Segunda Guerra Mundial se libró en el hemisferio norte, en lo que hoy se conoce como "mundo desarrollado", donde las economías de los países participantes se volcaron enteramente hacia la guerra. Toda la población y los recursos de Italia, Francia, Alemania, el Reino Unido, la Unión Soviética y EE.UU. estaban dedicados a suministrar armamento y munición a los combatientes.

Tanto los políticos como los generales reclamaban más aviones, barcos y tanques. En época de crisis, la cantidad es mucho más importante que la calidad. Con millones de hombres en los campos de combate, las mujeres desempeñaron un papel esencial en la producción de armamento.

Era necesario realizar tareas que antes hubieran parecido insólitas: apagar incendios, detectar aviones, dar alojamiento a niños y personas desplazadas, servir té y café a los soldados que regresaban a casa. Mujeres que hasta entonces habían servido en casas se encontraban ahora manejando armas antiaéreas, y hombres que salían de casa en traje para ir a trabajar ahora debían aprender a matar.

Cuando la guerra terminó y, por decirlo así, las espadas se convirtieron en arados, hubo que formar a millones de personas y volver a equipar las fábricas. La mayoría de las mujeres que habían trabajado en granjas y fábricas regresaron a los quehaceres domésticos.

Con l'eccezione del teatro del Pacifico la seconda guerra mondiale fu combattuta nell'emisfero settentrionale, in quello che oggi chiamiamo "mondo sviluppato". Intere economie di questa zona si convertirono alla produzione militare. Tutte le popolazioni e le risorse di Italia, Francia, Germania, Gran Bretagna, Unione Sovietica e Stati Uniti furono messe all'opera per fabbricare armi e munizioni.

Uomini politici e militari reclamavano all'unisono più aerei, più navi, più carri armati. In tempi di crisi la quantità era più importante della qualità. Mentre milioni di uomini combattevano al fronte, le donne adesso giocavano un ruolo chiave per garantire il rifornimento di armi.

Questo comportò l'assunzione di lavori che nessuno si sarebbe mai immaginato di fare prima: spegnere incendi, riparare aeroplani, preoccuparsi dei bambini e delle persone bisognose, preparare l'accoglienza per le truppe di ritorno dal fronte. Donne fino ad allora occupate in attività domestiche, si ritrovarono a guidare le batterie antiaeree, uomini fino ad allora occupati in mansioni "civili" impararono a uccidere.

Quando la guerra finì, e le spade rientrarono finalmente nei foderi, milioni di uomini dovettero essere rieducati, le fabbriche riconvertite. Le donne che avevano lavorato nelle fattorie e nelle industrie, in maggioranza, tornarono alle loro occupazioni domestiche.

Workers in a Lancashire factory stack barbed wire made from scrap metal. It was sent to France to protect the Allies from German invasion in 1940.

Obreros de una fábrica de Lancashire apilan rodillos de alambrada fabricados con metal reciclado. Después se enviarían a Francia para proteger a los aliados de la invasión alemana en 1940.

Operai di una fabbrica del Lancashire sistemano rotoli di filo spinato prodotto con materiale riciclato. Sarà mandato in Francia a protezione degli alleati dall'invasione tedesca del 1940.

Women munition-
workers in 1942.
In World War I
their mothers and
grandmothers would
probably have played
a less active role in
the war effort.

Obreras de una
fábrica de munición,
en 1942. En la
Primera Guerra
Mundial, sus madres
y abuelas
probablemente
desempeñaron un
papel menos activo
en la guerra.

Operaie in una
fabbrica di munizioni
nel 1942. Durante
la prima guerra
mondiale le loro
madri e nonne
avevano
probabilmente
giocato un ruolo
meno attivo negli
sforzi di guerra.

By 1940 the demand for women workers in Ministry of Supply factories was enormous. Churchill called for a million volunteers.

En 1940 la demanda de obreras para las fábricas del ministerio del aprovisionamiento era enorme. Churchill pidió a la población un millón de voluntarias.

Nel 1940 la domanda di operaie da utilizzare nelle fabbriche da parte del ministero per l'approvigionamento fu gigantesco. Churchill aveva richiesto un milione di volontarie.

Women were quick to learn the skills needed to produce weapons and ammunition. Here a woman is fitting the Caterpillar track on a tank. Her foreman may well have wondered what the world was coming to if he examined her footwear.

Las mujeres aprendían rápido las técnicas necesarias para fabricar armas y munición. En la foto, una mujer coloca la oruga de un tanque. Seguramente, el capataz de la fábrica se preguntaría hacia dónde iba el mundo al ver los zapatos que llevaba.

Le donne appresero rapidamente le tecniche per produrre armi e munizioni. Nella foto una donna monta dei cingoli su un carro armato. Il capo officina si domanderà certamente dove sta andando il mondo notando le scarpe che indossa l'operaia.

By 1941 Britain's railways were in crisis. They were having to carry goods that had previously travelled by sea, more passengers than ever before (as a result of petrol rationing), and weapons of war from the factories in the north to the ports in the south.

En 1941 los ferrocarriles británicos estaban en crisis. Tenían que transportar productos que antes hubieran viajado por mar, más pasajeros que nunca hasta entonces (como consecuencia del racionamiento del carburante) y toneladas de armamento, desde las fábricas del norte hasta los puertos del sur.

Nel 1941 le ferrovie inglesi erano in piena crisi. Dovevano trasportare i beni che prima viaggiavano per nave, un maggior numero di passeggeri rispetto al passato (a causa del razionamento del carburante), e inoltre dovevano portare le armi prodotte dalle fabbriche del Nord fino ai porti del Sud.

Lancaster bombers are assembled at a factory near Manchester,
September 1943. They were the first of the long-range British
bombers, and were used to attack targets deep in enemy territory.

Montaje de bombarderos Lancaster en una fábrica cerca de
Manchester, en septiembre de 1943. Eran los primeros
bombarderos británicos de largo alcance, que se utilizaron para
atacar objetivos situados en el corazón del territorio enemigo.

Montaggio di bombardieri Lancaster in una fabbrica vicino a
Manchester, settembre 1943. Furono i primi bombardieri
britannici a lungo raggio usati per colpire bersagli nel cuore
del territorio nemico.

Primitive methods, modern weapons. War workers add explosives to bomb casings. The British munitions industry lived a hand-to-mouth existence in 1940.

Métodos primitivos, armas modernas. Dos obreras vierten explosivos en carcasas de bombas. En 1940, la industria británica de producción de municiones era extremadamente precaria.

Metodi primitivi, armi moderne. Operaie di guerra versano esplosivo nel cilindro di una bomba. L'industria di munizioni britannica nel 1940 era estremamente precaria.

Keep fit exercises, 1941 style. A woman casually rolls a bomb across the factory floor in Bert Hardy's photograph.

Ejercicios para mantenerse en forma, al estilo de 1941. Una mujer hace rodar despreocupadamente una bomba por el suelo de una fábrica. La fotografía es de Bert Hardy.

Fare ginnastica alla moda del 1941. Una donna fa elegantemente rotolare una bomba sul pavimento della fabbrica in una foto di Bert Hardy.

German children play among rows of shells awaiting collection in a Munich street, May 1943. It wasn't until after 1943 that Allied bombing made any significant reduction in German manufacture and production of war materials.

Unas niñas alemanas juegan entre carcasas de obuses antes de ser éstas recogidas en una calle de Múnich, en mayo de 1943. Hasta después de este año, los bombardeos aliados no consiguieron reducir de forma significativa la producción de material de guerra alemana.

Bambini tedeschi giocano vicino a bombe in attesa di essere raccolte in una strada di Monaco, maggio 1943. I bombardamenti alleati riuscirono soltanto a partire dal 1943 a frenare la produzione di armi in Germania.

Hand grenades on an assembly line in Moscow, 1942.
The Soviet Union ran a quota system for each factory,
challenging workers to exceed the production expected
of them.

Granadas de mano en una cadena de montaje de Moscú,
en 1942. La Unión Soviética instauró un sistema de
cuotas en las fábricas para estimular la producción.

Montaggio di granate in una fabbrica di Mosca nel
1942. L'Unione Sovietica instaura un sistema di quote
per ciascuna fabbrica, incitando gli operai a superare la
produzione così stabilita.

Russian women grease artillery shells by hand before dispatch to the front. In 1942 the Soviet Union was fighting for its very existence, with Leningrad and Stalingrad besieged, and Moscow itself under threat.

Mujeres rusas engrasan con sus manos obuses de artillería destinados al frente. En 1942, la Unión Soviética luchaba por su propia existencia, con Leningrado y Stalingrado sitiadas y Moscú bajo amenaza.

Donne russe ingrassano a mano proiettili per l'artiglieria prima dell'invio al fronte. Nel 1942 l'Unione Sovietica combatteva per la sua stessa sopravvivenza, con Leningrado e Stalingrado sotto assedio e la stessa Mosca seriamente minacciata.

In 1940, rifles that the British troops of 1914 would have recognized are stacked from a wheelbarrow at the Royal Ordnance Factory. Many months were to pass before the British supply system reached the required efficiency.

En 1940, unos rifles que los soldados de 1914 habrían reconocido de inmediato son descargados de una carretilla en la Royal Ordnance Factory. Pasaron muchos meses antes de que el sistema de producción británico alcanzara la eficacia necesaria.

Nel 1940 fucili che le truppe britanniche del 1914 avrebbero riconosciuto a prima vista, vengono caricati su una carriola alla Royal Ordnance Factory. Dovevano passare ancora molti mesi prima che il sistema di approvvigionamento britannico raggiungesse l'efficienza richiesta.

A Canadian worker fits transparent hoods over the landing lights of Harvard monoplanes. Many Commonwealth pilots trained on the Harvard.

Un obrero canadiense monta cubiertas transparentes sobre las luces de aterrizaje de monoplanos Harvard. Muchos pilotos de la Commonwealth se entrenaron en este tipo de aviones.

Un operaio canadese monta un paraluce trasparente sui fari d'atterraggio di un Harvard. Molti piloti del Commonwealth si addestrarono sugli Harvard.

London firemen pack the galleries to watch the final of the Auxiliary
Fire Service trailer pump competition, March 1940. A tougher
test was to come for the AFS later that year when the Blitz began.

Bomberos londinenses abarrotan los balcones para ver la final del
campeonato de gimnasia del cuerpo auxiliar de bomberos, en marzo
de 1940. Las pruebas verdaderamente difíciles llegarían apenas un año
después, cuando empezó el *Blitz,* los ataques aéreos sobre Londres.

Pompieri londinesi ai balconi assistono alla finale del concorso di
ginnastica dei pompieri ausiliari nel marzo 1940. Una prova ben più
difficile li aspettava pochi mesi più tardi con l'inizio dei
bombardamenti del Blitz tedesco.

Fitness training
before the Battle of
Britain. Young
RAF recruits keep
their guard up,
February 1940.

Entrenamiento antes
de la Batalla de
Inglaterra. Jóvenes
reclutas de la RAF
practicando el boxeo
en febrero de 1940.

Educazione fisica
prima della battaglia
d'Inghilterra.
Giovani reclute della
RAF si mettono in
guardia, febbraio
1940.

What a way to win a war! Royal Air Force cadets learn the art of formation flying on bicycles, June 1942. No matter how hard they pedalled, the wings were never large enough to enable them to take off.

¡Qué forma de ganar una guerra! Cadetes de la RAF aprenden a volar en formación utilizando bicicletas, en junio de 1942. Aunque pedaleasen con todas sus fuerzas, las alas que llevan son demasiado pequeñas para poder despegar.

Ma che modo di vincere la guerra! I cadetti dalla Royal Air Force imparano a volare in formazione con l'aiuto di biciclette, giugno 1942. Anche se avessero pedalato molto velocemente la ridotta dimensione delle ali non avrebbe consentito loro di volare.

A sporting chance. RAF gunners train by aiming their gun at a moving target. Unsportingly, German Fokkers and Messerschmitts tended to appear out of the clouds moving considerably faster.

El juego de la guerra. Artilleros de la RAF se entrenan apuntando con la metralleta a un objetivo móvil. Con un espíritu mucho menos deportivo, los Fokkers y Messerschmitts alemanes solían aparecer por sorpresa de entre las nubes y a bastante mayor velocidad.

Pronti, mirate, fuoco! Artiglieri dalla RAF imparano a mirare su un bersaglio mobile. Poco sportivamente i Fokker e i Messerschmitt tedeschi erano soliti sbucare dalle nuvole a una velocità molto maggiore.

Fit for battle. Much of the basic training of recruits was concerned with improving physical fitness. The emphasis on precision was often an attempt to keep morale high. Rivalry between different units was sometimes fiercer than hatred of the enemy.

En forma para la batalla. Buena parte de la formación básica de los reclutas consistía en mejorar su estado físico. El énfasis en la precisión tenía a menudo el objetivo de mantener alta la moral. A veces, la rivalidad entre las diversas unidades era mayor que el odio al enemigo.

In forma per la battaglia. Gran parte dell'addestramento delle reclute si concentrava sul miglioramento delle prestazioni fisiche. L'accento posto sulla precisione era spesso un tentativo di mantenere alto il morale. La rivalità tra le diverse unità era talvolta più pronunciata dell'odio verso lo stesso nemico.

A gymnastic
display by soldiers
recovering at a
military
convalescence
depot in south-east
England, 1940,

Una exhibición de
gimnasia realizada
por soldados
convalescentes
de un centro de
recuperación militar
del sureste de
Inglaterra, en 1940.

Una prova di
ginnastica di soldati
ricoverati in un
centro per
convalescenti militari
nell'Inghilterra
sudorientale, 1940.

4. Heading for peace
Avanzando hacia la paz
Avanzando verso la pace

Paul Tibbets waves from the cockpit of *Enola Gay*, the B-29 Superfortress that dropped the first atomic bomb on Japan. The plane was named after Tibbets' mother. The bomb wiped out four square miles (10 square kilometres) of Hiroshima.

Paul Tibbets saluda desde la cabina del *Enola Gay*, la superfortaleza B-29 que arrojó la primera bomba atómica sobre Japón. El avión fue bautizado con el nombre de la madre de Tibbets. La bomba redujo a cenizas diez kilómetros cuadrados de Hiroshima.

Paul Tibbets saluta dalla cabina di *Enola Gay*, il B-29 che lancerà la prima bomba atomica sul Giappone. L'aereo fu battezzato con il nome della madre di Tibbets. La bomba spazzò via 10 chilometri quadrati di Hiroshima.

4. Heading for peace
Avanzando hacia la paz
Avanzando verso la pace

The tide of war turned. It became not a question of who would win, but how long the losers could keep going. Village by village across Normandy, more rapidly across great swathes of Eastern Europe, the fighting pushed closer to Berlin. Mussolini's strutting reign in Italy came to a shocking end. City after city, camp after camp was liberated from Fascist control.

Partisans hastened the process. Gradually they ceased to be silent, secret organizations that struck by night. They emerged into the open, taking over increasingly large sections of their homeland as the occupying troops retreated.

In the Far East the sun began to sink over the Japanese empire. The fighting here was some of the bitterest in the whole war – every island became a battleground, losses on both sides were appalling. And then came the final monstrous explosions that dealt a death-blow to the guilty and the innocent alike.

Briefly, there were heady days of celebration for the victors. But only in the immediate aftermath did people begin to grasp just how terrible the war had been. As survivors trickled out of camps of death, the world at last witnessed the extent of the evil that had been unleashed, confronted and finally beaten.

La marea de la guerra estaba bajando. La cuestión ya no era quién ganaría, sino cuánto tiempo aguantarían los perdedores. Pueblo a pueblo en Normandía, más rápidamente en las vastas regiones de Europa oriental, los combates se iban acercando a Berlín. El infame gobierno de Mussolini en Italia tuvo un final dramático. Ciudad tras ciudad, campo tras campo, el viejo continente iba siendo liberado del yugo fascista.

Los partisanos contribuyeron a acelerar el proceso. Poco a poco, dejaron de ser organizaciones secretas y silenciosas que actuaban de noche y salieron a la luz, haciéndose con el control de zonas cada vez más extensas a medida que las tropas de ocupación se retiraban.

En Extremo Oriente, el sol empezó a ponerse en el imperio japonés. Los combates librados en esta zona fueron quizá los más sangrientos de toda la guerra. Cada isla era un campo de batalla, las bajas en ambos bandos fueron innumerables y, finalmente, llegaron las monstruosas explosiones que sembraron la muerte entre culpables e inocentes por igual.

En seguida llegaron los eufóricos días de celebración para los ganadores. Pero poco a poco la gente empezó a comprender lo terrible que había sido la guerra. A medida que los supervivientes abandonaban los campos de exterminio, el mundo se fue dando cuenta del infierno que se había desatado, combatido y, finalmente, vencido.

La guerra giunge a una svolta. È ormai chiaro chi vincerà, si tratta di capire quanto ancora potrà resistere. Conquistando villaggio su villaggio attraverso la Normandia, e ancor più rapidamente nelle vaste pianure dell'Europa orientale, i combattimenti si avvicinano a Berlino. L'arrogante dominio di Mussolini in Italia fa una fine ignobile. Città dopo città, campo dopo campo, l'Italia è liberata dal giogo fascista.

I partigiani accelerano il processo. Gradualmente smettono di essere associazioni clandestine e silenziose che colpiscono nella notte e cominciano a operare alla luce del sole, liberando una parte sempre più ampia del paese a mano a mano che le truppe di occupazione si ritirano.

In Estremo Oriente il sole comincia a tramontare sull'impero giapponese. I combattimenti furono qui tra i più aspri di tutta la guerra: ogni isola diventò un campo di battaglia, con spaventose perdite per entrambe le parti. Le mostruose esplosioni finali causarono la morte tanto dei colpevoli quanto degli innocenti.

Alla fine, ci furono inebrianti giornate di allegria per i vincitori. Ma immediatamente dopo la guerra la gente cominciò a capire quanto terrificante fosse stata quell'esperienza. Allorché i sopravvissuti uscirono dai campi di sterminio, il mondo poté misurare l'enormità del male al quale ci si era oppposti, con il quale ci si era confrontati e che, alla fine, era stato sconfitto.

April 1945. Dead and dying prisoners huddled together
in the concentration camp at Nordhausen, Germany,
50 miles west of Leipzig. They were found lying on straw
by members of the American First Army.

Abril de 1945. Prisioneros muertos y moribundos hacinados
en el campo de concentración de Nordhausen, en Alemania,
a 80 kilómetros al oeste de Leipzig. Los soldados del primer
ejército estadounidense les encontraron tendidos sobre paja.

Aprile 1945. Prigionieri morti o in agonia nel campo di
concentramento di Nordhausen, 80 chilometri a ovest di
Lipsia. Furono trovati da membri della I armata americana
abbandonati sulla paglia.

The entrance to the camp at Terezin. The slogan above the gate reads, 'Work Makes You Free'.

La entrada del campo de Terezin. Sobre la puerta puede leerse: "El trabajo os hará libres".

L'ingresso del campo di concentramento di Terezin. La scritta sopra la porta asserisce: "Il lavoro rende liberi".

By the end of the war the Nazis had established dozens of concentration camps in Germany, Poland and Austria, including the so-called 'death camps' – extermination centres designed to kill entire populations. But thousands of prisoners survived.

Hacia el final de la guerra, los nazis habían construido decenas de campos de concentración en Alemania, Polonia y Austria, incluidos los llamados "campos de la muerte", centros de exterminio destinados a eliminar poblaciones enteras. A pesar de todo, miles de prisioneros lograron sobrevivir.

Fino alla fine della guerra i nazisti avevano creato decine di campi di concentramento in Germania, Polonia e Austria, compresi i cosiddetti "campi della morte" – centri di sterminio destinati all'eliminazione di intere popolazioni. Migliaia di prigionieri riuscirono comunque a sopravvivere.

A death pit at Bergen-Belsen, 1945. Prisoners were usually kept alive for six weeks, though many died of malnutrition or illness during that time. At the end of the six weeks, most survivors were brutally slaughtered.

Una fosa común en Bergen-Belsen, en 1945. Generalmente, a los prisioneros se les mantenía vivos durante seis semanas, aunque durante este período muchos morían de hambre o enfermedad. Transcurrido este tiempo, la mayoría de los supervivientes eran asesinados brutalmente.

Una fossa comune a Bergen-Belsen, nel 1945. I prigionieri venivano generalmente tenuti in vita per sei settimane, anche se moltissimi non sopravvivevano, per denutrizione e malattie, a questo periodo. Alla fine delle sei settimane la maggior parte dei sopravvissuti veniva brutalmente trucidata.

Buchenwald Camp, May 1945. Prisoners were stripped of anything valuable before being led to the gas chambers – that included gold fillings from their teeth, and, in this case, their wedding rings.

El campo de Buchenwald, en mayo de 1945. A los prisioneros se les despojaba de todos sus objetos de valor, como dientes de oro y anillos de matrimonio, antes de conducirles a las cámaras de gas.

Campo di concentramento di Buchenwald, nel maggio 1945. I prigionieri venivano derubati di qualsiasi bene di valore prima di essere inviati nelle camere a gas – comprese le otturazioni in oro dei denti e, in questo caso, le fedi.

German civilians from nearby are forced to witness the horrors of Buchenwald Camp, 1945. The camp, near Weimar in central Germany, was established in the 1930s.

Ciudadanos alemanes de las poblaciones de alrededor son obligados a contemplar los horrores del campo de concentración de Buchenwald, en 1945. Este campo, cerca de Weimar, en el centro de Alemania, se construyó en la década de 1930.

Civili tedeschi vengono costretti ad assistere agli orrori del campo di Buchenwald, nel 1945. Il campo, prossimo a Weimar, nel cuore della Germania, era stato costruito durante gli anni Trenta.

German civilians were taken to the death camps immediately after liberation. They were shown, together with the rest of the world, how the prisoners met their deaths, how their corpses were transported, and how they were buried.

Inmediatamente después de la liberación, muchos ciudadanos alemanes fueron conducidos a los campos de exterminio para que, junto con el resto del mundo, pudieran ver con sus propios ojos cómo murieron los prisioneros, cómo se transportaban sus cuerpos y cómo se les enterraba.

Civili tedeschi vengono condotti in un campo di sterminio immediatamente dopo la liberazione. A essi, e al resto del mondo, veniva mostrato come i prigionieri andavano incontro alla morte, come venivano trasportati e come venivano sepolti.

May 1945. American editors and publishers witness the horrors of Dachau Camp. The group includes Norman Chandler (*LA Times*), Julius Adler (*NY Times*), M E Walker (*Houston Chronicle*), William Nichols (*This Week*), E Z Dimitman (*Chicago Sun*), William Chenery (*Colliers*) and L K Nicholson (*NO Times*).

Mayo de 1945. Editores y periodistas estadounidenses son testigos de los horrores del campo de Dachau. El grupo está formado por Norman Chandler *(LA Times)*, Julius Adler *(NY Times)*, M.E. Walker *(Houston Chronicle)*, William Nichols *(This Week)*, E.Z. Dimitman *(Chicago Sun)*, William Chenery *(Colliers)* y L.K. Nicholson *(NO Times)*.

Maggio 1945. Alcuni editori e giornalisti americani assistono agli orrori di Dachau. Il gruppo comprende Norman Chandler (*LA Times*), Julius Adler (*NY Times*), M. E. Walker (*Houston Chronicle*), William Nichols (*This Week*), E. Z. Dimitman (*Chicago Sun*), William Chenery (*Colliers*) et L. K. Nicholson (*NO Times*).

As Allied armies advanced deeper into mainland Europe, partisan groups emerged from the woods and mountains to reclaim their own cities. Here an Italian group associated with the Partito d'Azione patrol the streets of Milan early in 1945.

A medida que las tropas aliadas avanzaban hacia el corazón de Europa, los grupos de partisanos salían de los bosques y las montañas para reconquistar sus ciudades. En la foto, un grupo italiano relacionado con el Partito d'Azione patrulla por las calles de Milán a principios de 1945.

Mentre gli alleati avanzavano sempre più profondamente nel cuore dell'Europa, dai boschi e dalle montagne uscivano gruppi di partigiani per andare a liberare le proprie città. Nella foto un gruppo di partigiani appartenenti al Partito d'Azione pattuglia le strade di Milano all'inizio del 1945.

June 1944. A French Resistance fighter in Chateaudun holds a gun designed by the Czechs and supplied by the British.

Junio de 1944. Un combatiente de la resistencia francesa en Chateaudun, con un rifle fabricado en Checoslovaquia y proporcionado por los británicos.

Giugno 1944. Un membro della resistenza francese, a Chateaudun, impugna un fucile fabbricato in Cecoslovacchia e paracadutato dai britannici.

August 1944. Members of the French Resistance mopping up
a Paris street. There were those among the Allies who hoped that
the French would rid the city of German troops on their own. But
there were others who fought to be the first to enter Paris.

Agosto de 1944. Miembros de la Resistencia francesa limpiando
una calle de París. Entre los aliados, algunos esperaban que los
franceses lograran expulsar de la ciudad a los alemanes por sí
solos, pero otros lucharon por ser los primeros en entrar en París.

Agosto 1944. Partigiani francesi rastrellano una via di Parigi.
C'erano tra gli alleati alcuni che speravano che i francesi avrebbero
liberato da soli la città dalle truppe tedesche. Altri invece si
batterono per essere i primi a entrare a Parigi.

The day of reckoning, France. A French woman (in dark dress) and man (in white shirt) plead their innocence in front of members of the local Resistance. The couple are accused of spying for the Gestapo. They are unlikely to be shown any mercy.

El día de la revancha en Francia. Una francesa (con vestido negro) y un hombre (con camisa blanca) defienden su inocencia ante miembros de la Resistencia local. Se les acusa de ser espías de la Gestapo. Difícilmente se les concederá clemencia.

Il giorno della vendetta, Francia. Una donna (col vestito scuro) e un uomo (con la camicia bianca) francesi giurano la loro innocenza di fronte a membri della resistenza locale. La coppia era accusata di essere spia della Gestapo. È poco probabile che abbiano avuto un atteggiamento di clemenza nei loro confronti.

August 1944. A proud group of French locals escort a German prisoner. The man was a member of the SS who had fallen behind when the German army retreated from Chartres. For him, there may be some mercy, as a prisoner of war.

Agosto de 1944. Un grupo de franceses escolta con aires de venganza a un prisionero alemán, un miembro de la SS que quedó rezagado cuando el ejército alemán se retiró de Chartres. Al tratarse de un prisionero de guerra, es posible que se le conceda clemencia.

Agosto 1944. Un fiero gruppo di francesi scorta un prigioniero tedesco. L'uomo era un membro delle SS che era rimasto dietro le retrovie quando l'esercito tedesco si era ritirato da Chartres. In quanto prigioniero di guerra, era stato probabilmente "risparmiato".

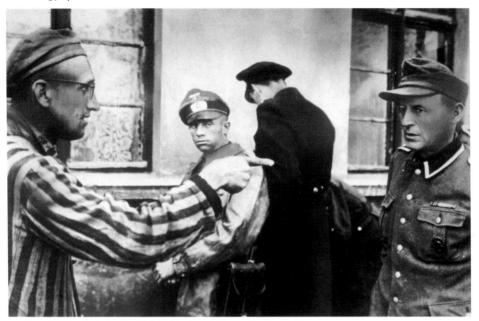

The day of reckoning, Germany. A Russian slave labourer identifies a former Nazi guard and accuses him of brutally beating prisoners. The camp had just been liberated by the American First Army.

El día de la venganza en Alemania. Un ruso obligado a realizar trabajos forzados identifica a un antiguo guardia nazi y le acusa de haber pegado brutalmente a los prisioneros. La foto está tomada en un campo de concentración recién liberado por el primer ejército estadounidense.

Il giorno della vendetta, Germania. Un lavoratore forzato russo identifica una ex guardia nazista e lo accusa di di avere brutalmente bastonato i prigionieri. Il campo era appena stato liberato dalla I armata americana.

A group of French women, one with her head shorn, are paraded in public shame. They had been accused of collaborating with German occupying troops. Publication of photographs like this led to an outcry, and the humiliation was stopped.

Un grupo de francesas, una con la cabeza rapada, obligadas a ir en ropa interior para humillarlas ante el público. Se las acusa de haber colaborado con las tropas de ocupación alemanas. La publicación de fotografías como ésta suscitó indignación, lo que llevó a detener este tipo de prácticas.

Un gruppo di donne francesi, tra le quali una con la testa rasata, è esposto al dileggio pubblico. Sono accusate di avere collaborato con le truppe d'occupazione tedesche. La pubblicazione di fotografie come questa suscitò indignazione e pose fine al ripetersi di episodi del genere.

A German prisoner of war hurries through a street in Toulon, France, on his way to camp. The following jeep will probably ensure he arrives bruised but alive.

Un prisionero de guerra alemán corre por una calle de Toulon, Francia, hacia el campo de concentración. El vehículo que le sigue se encarga de garantizar que llegue vivo a su destino, aunque sea lleno de morados.

Un prigioniero tedesco corre per una strada di Tolone, in Francia, per raggiungere il campo. La jeep che lo segue probabilmente ne garantirà l'arrivo, ammaccato ma vivo.

A final reckoning.
A young Frenchman,
found guilty
of treason, is tied
to a stake before
execution.

Venganza final.
Un joven francés,
culpable de traición,
es atado a un poste
para ser ejecutado.

Vendetta finale.
Un giovane francese
accusato di
tradimento viene
legato a un palo
poco prima
dell'esecuzione.

In the little village of Sainte-Mère l'Eglise, two miles from the landing stage of Utah Beach, an elderly Frenchwoman welcomes an American military policeman to what is left of her home.

En el pequeño pueblo de Sainte-Mère l'Eglise, a cuatro kilómetros del lugar donde tuvo lugar el desembarco de Utah Beach, una anciana francesa da la bienvenida a un policía militar estadounidense y le invita a entrar en lo que queda de su casa.

Nel piccolo villaggio di Sainte-Mère-l'Eglise, a quattro chilometri dal luogo di sbarco di Utah Beach, un'anziana francese accoglie un membro della polizia militare americana davanti alle rovine della sua casa.

August 1944. A member of General Leclerc's Second French Armoured
Division, the first Allied troops to enter Paris, leads German prisoners
past the Arc de Triomphe. The Tricolour flies once more.

Agosto de 1944. Un miembro de la segunda división blindada francesa
del general Leclerc, las primeras tropas aliadas que entraron en París,
obliga a un grupo de prisioneros alemanes a pasar bajo el Arco de
Triunfo. La bandera tricolor vuelve a ondear sobre la capital.

Agosto 1944. Un membro della Seconda divisione blindata francese
del generale Leclerc, le prime truppe alleate a entrare a Parigi, guida un
gruppo di prigionieri tedeschi attraverso l'Arco di trionfo. Il tricolore
torna a sventolare sulla capitale.

Ecstatic Parisians crowd the streets to
cheer American troops, August 1944.
Perhaps, in the long run, it didn't matter
too much which troops liberated Paris.

Los parisinos, eufóricos, abarrotan las
calles de la ciudad para dar la bienvenida
a los soldados estadounidenses, en agosto
de 1944. Visto desde la distancia, en el
fondo a nadie le importaba demasiado
qué tropas liberaran París.

Una folla entusiasta di parigini accoglie
le truppe americane, agosto 1944. Senza
dubbio, a qualche anno di distanza non
sarà più importante sapere quali truppe
hanno liberato la città.

German stragglers and sympathizers were still active in the early days of the liberation of Paris. The city was not yet a safe place. French gendarmes and civilians take cover as a sniper fires down into the street.

En los primeros años tras la liberación de París, aún se veían alemanes rezagados y simpatizantes. La ciudad todavía no era un lugar seguro. En la foto, gendarmes y ciudadanos se cubren de los disparos de un francotirador.

Franchi tiratori tedeschi e simpatizzanti erano ancora attivi nei giorni immediatamente successivi alla liberazione di Parigi. La città non era ancora un luogo sicuro. Gendarmi e civili francesi, presi di mira da un franco tiratore, cercano riparo dietro le auto.

The calm after the storm. Soviet troops chat to local
women somewhere in Germany, 1945. The scene is
peaceful and friendly. Perhaps they were all as conscious
of the camera as the young soldier on the left.

Momentos de calma tras la tormenta. Soldados soviéticos
hablan con un grupo de mujeres en algún lugar de
Alemania, en 1945. La imagen desprende paz y alegría.
Seguro que todos eran tan conscientes de la presencia de
la cámara como el soldado de la izquierda.

La quiete dopo la tempesta. Soldati sovietici chiacchierano
con alcune donne locali in un luogo imprecisato in
Germania nel 1945. La scena è pacifica e amichevole.
Probabilmente, come dimostra il giovane in primo piano,
erano consci di essere ripresi.

London, July 1944. In the West End, special clubs were set aside for the use of black US troops. This was at the request of the American authorities. It did not occur to the majority of Londoners, at this time, that black and white should be segregated.

Londres, julio de 1944. En el West End se abrieron clubes especiales para los soldados estadounidenses de color, a petición de las autoridades norteamericanas. En esa época, la mayoría de los londinenses la segregación racial les parecía algo verdaderamente extraño.

Londra, luglio 1944. Nel West End, su richiesta del comando americano, si aprirono locali speciali per le truppe di colore. A quei tempi però la maggioranza dei londinesi era indifferente a questo tipo di segregazione razziale.

Piccadilly Circus, December 1942. American troops play free pinball machines at the American Red Cross Club.

Piccadilly Circus, en diciembre de 1942. Soldados estadounidenses juegan a las máquinas del millón en el club de la Cruz Roja norteamericana.

Piccadilly Circus, dicembre 1942. Soldati americani giocano a flipper al circolo della Croce Rossa americana.

The Club was known as Rainbow Corner. It was an attempt to bring a touch of the United States to troops thousands of miles from home. Prizes for playing the machines were hardly on a Las Vegas scale. The best you could get was a pack of cigarettes.

Este club, conocido con el nombre de Rainbow Corner, se creó para intentar que los soldados estadounidenses, a miles de kilómetros de su país, se sintieran como en casa. Los premios que podían conseguirse no tenían nada que ver con los de Las Vegas. El premio mayor era un paquete de cigarrillos.

Il circolo era noto come Rainbow Corner. Rappresentava il tentativo di portare un po' d'aria di casa a soldati americani lontani migliaia di chilometri dalla loro patria. I premi che le macchinette distribuivano non erano però paragonabili a quelli di Las Vegas. Nel migliore dei casi si vinceva un pacchetto di sigarette.

The noble art of fraternization. Once the fighting stopped, it wasn't long before Allied troops began 'fratting', as here in a wood on the outskirts of Berlin. The soldiers were far from home, and a generation of German men had perished in the war.

El noble arte del flirteo. Una vez terminados los combates, los soldados aliados en seguida empezaron a "confraternizar", en escenarios tan idílicos como este bosque de las afueras de Berlín. Los soldados estaban lejos de casa y toda una generación de alemanes había perecido en la guerra.

La nobile arte della fraternizzazione. Già poco tempo dopo il termine delle ostilità, i militari cominciarono a "fraternizzare", come in questa foto in un bosco nei dintorni di Berlino. I soldati erano lontani da casa e tutta una generazione di uomini tedeschi era morta durante la guerra.

Although frowned upon by some, the often short-lived romances between Allied troops and German women helped momentarily to relieve some of the bitterness of six long years.

Aunque algunos los criticaban, los romances entre soldados aliados y mujeres alemanas, a menudo de corta duración, ayudaron momentáneamente a olvidar el sufrimiento de seis largos años.

Anche se criticate da alcuni, le spesso effimere storie d'amore tra militari americani e giovani donne tedesche aiutarono a mitigare, almeno per un po', l'orrore di sei lunghi anni di guerra.

German soldiers are rounded up by American
troops on the streets of Aachen. The war
in all its misery had come home to Germany.

Soldados alemanes registrados por las tropas
estadounidenses en las calles de Aquisgrán.
La guerra, con todas sus miserias, había
llegado a territorio alemán.

Soldati tedeschi vengono circondati da
militari americani nelle strade di Aquisgrana.
La guerra in tutta la sua miseria era penetrata
entro i confini della Germania.

An international misunderstanding: the Russian soldier believes the woman's bicycle was for sale. It isn't. She struggles to keep this precious belonging. It happened in Berlin. It could have been in any German city.

Un malentendido internacional: un soldado ruso cree que la bicicleta de esta mujer está en venta. No lo está y la mujer lucha para conservar tan valiosa pertenencia. La escena tiene lugar en Berlín, pero podría haber sucedido en cualquier ciudad de Alemania.

Un'incomprensione internazionale: il soldato russo crede che la bicicletta della donna sia in vendita. La donna, invece, si batte per conservare la preziosa proprietà. La scena si svolge a Berlino, ma si sarebbe potuta verificare in qualsiasi altra città della Germania.

The Victory Two-Step. Russian and American troops dance together after their respective armies meet in a German town. Within a few years the same soldiers could have been facing each other on either side of the Iron Curtain.

Unos compases para celebrar la victoria. Un soldado ruso y uno estadounidense bailan juntos después de que sus respectivos ejércitos se encontraran en una ciudad de Alemania. Pocos años más tarde, los mismos soldados podrían haberse vuelto a encontrar, esta vez uno a cada lado del telón de acero.

Un balletto per la vittoria. Militari russi e americani ballano insieme dopo che le rispettive unità si sono incontrate in un villaggio tedesco. Solo pochi anni dopo gli stessi soldati si sarebbero potuti trovare ai lati opposti della cortina di ferro.

An historic handshake on 27 April 1945. Infantrymen of the American First Army meet Soviet soldiers on the remains of the bridge over the Elbe at Torgau, near Leipzig. Hitler had three days to live.

Un histórico apretón de manos, el 27 de abril de 1945. Soldados de infantería del primer ejército alemán saludan a soldados rusos sobre las ruinas del puente sobre el Elba en Torgau, cerca de Leipzig. A Hitler le quedaban tres días de vida.

Una storica stretta di mano il 27 aprile 1945. Fanti della I armata americana incontrano i soldati sovietici sulle rovine del ponte sull'Elba a Torgau, nei pressi di Lipsia. A Hitler non restavano che tre giorni di vita.

Perhaps the most famous picture ever taken by Russian photographer Yevgeny Khaldei. It was taken on 30 April 1945, the day Hitler committed suicide, and shows the Red Flag being hoisted by Russian soldiers over the ruins of the Reichstag in Berlin.

Esta es sin duda la imagen más famosa tomada por el fotógrafo ruso Yevgueni Khaldei, el 30 de abril de 1945, el día que Hitler se suicidó. En ella, soldados rusos enarbolan la bandera roja sobre las ruinas del Reichstag de Berlín.

Forse la più celebre immagine del fotografo russo Yevgeny Khaldei. La fotografia fu scattata il 30 aprile 1945, il giorno in cui Hitler si suicidò, e mostra soldati russi che sventolano la bandiera rossa sulle rovine del Reichstag a Berlino.

US paratroopers display a Nazi flag captured in an assault on a French village, not long after the D-day landings. The creases on the flag suggest that it has already been carefully folded and kept in a trooper's backpack. Its destination is certainly the United States.

Paracaidistas estadounidenses muestran una bandera nazi capturada en un asalto a una población francesa, unos días después de los desembarcos del día D. Los pliegues que se observan indican que ya se había dablado y guardado cuidadosamente en una mochila, para enviarla a EE.UU.

Paracadutisti americani mostrano una bandiera nazista catturata durante l'assalto di un villaggio francese, qualche giorno dopo il D-day. Le pieghe sulla bandiera lasciano immaginare che sia già stata accuratamente piegata e conservata nella sacca di un soldato. Il luogo di destinazione sarà certamente gli Stati Uniti.

Meanwhile in the Pacific, other American troops hold a bullet-torn Japanese flag, captured at Eniwetok in the Marshall Islands.

Mientras tanto, en el Pacífico, otros soldados estadounidenses sostienen una bandera japonesa con agujeros de bala capturada en Eniwetok, en las islas Marshall.

Nello stesso tempo, nel Pacifico, altri militari americani recuperano una bandiera giapponese perforata dai proiettili e conquistata a Eniwetok, nelle isole Marshall.

The mixed fortunes of war: Allied victories. American troops
escort Japanese prisoners from the front line as the US forces drive
back the enemy, advancing island by island across the Pacific.

Las diversas suertes de la guerra: aliados victoriosos. Soldados
estadounidenses escoltan a prisioneros japoneses en el frente
mientras las tropas norteamericanas hacen retroceder al enemigo
avanzando isla a isla en el Pacífico.

Fortune diverse in guerra: vittorie alleate. Militari americani
scortano i prigionieri giapponesi dalle linee del fronte, mentre
l'esercito americano avanza isola per isola attraverso il Pacifico,
respingendo indietro il nemico.

Allied defeats. In the same theatre of war, just a year or two earlier, American and Philippine troops surrender to the Japanese on the island of Bataan.

Aliados derrotados. En el mismo escenario bélico, tan sólo uno o dos años antes, soldados estadounidenses y filipinos se rinden a los japoneses en la isla de Bataan.

Sconfitte alleate. Nello stesso teatro di guerra, non più di uno o due anni prima, militari americani e filippini si arrendono ai giapponesi nell'isola di Bataan.

Chinese soldiers
guard a Japanese
prisoner at Changteh
in the province
of Hunan, 1944.

Soldados chinos
custodian a un
prisionero japonés
en Changteh, en la
provincia de Hunan,
en 1944.

Soldati cinesi
montano la guardia
a un prigioniero
giapponese
a Changteh, nella
provincia di Hunan,
nel 1944.

After the flag was raised on the Japanese island of Iwo Jima,
American troops surround Japanese soldiers taken prisoner. It took
four days of bitter fighting for the Americans to gain control.

Tras izar la bandera en la isla japonesa de Iwo Jima, varios soldados
estadounidenses rodean a unos soldados japoneses tomados
prisioneros. Fueron necesarios cuatro días de duros combates para
controlar la isla.

Dopo che la bandiera americana è stata issata nell'isola giapponese
di Iwo Jima, militari americani circondano soldati giapponesi fatti
prigionieri. Ci vollero quattro giorni di durissima battaglia perché
gli americani prendessero il controllo dell'isola.

10 August 1945. The day the Japanese offered to surrender.
American troops and a British Wren (Women's Royal Navy Service)
cheer a member of the Chinese Military Mission in Piccadilly Circus.

10 de agosto de 1945. El día de la rendición del Japón. Soldados
estadounidenses y una británica del WREN (Women's Royal Navy
Service), aúpan a un miembro de la Misión Militar China en
Piccadilly Circus.

10 agosto 1945. Il giorno in cui i giapponesi chiedono la resa.
Militari americani e una Wren (Women's Royal Navy Service)
festeggiano un membro della Missione militare cinese a Piccadilly
Circus.

On the same day in the same city, a group of Chinese waiters read the news of Japan's surrender. The two-finger 'Victory V' sign has been reversed, but it is no doubt intended as a gesture of celebration.

Ese mismo día, en la misma ciudad, un grupo de chinos lee en el periódico que Japón se ha rendido. Aunque hacen el símbolo de la victoria con la mano al revés, no cabe duda de que celebran la noticia.

Lo stesso giorno nella stessa città, un gruppo di camerieri cinesi legge la notizia della resa giapponese. Le due dita che simboleggiano la V della vittoria sono al contrario, ma non c'è dubbio che esse esprimono un gesto di gioia.

Loudspeakers are fitted in Trafalgar Square for a victory speech by King George VI. May brought the end of the war in Europe, but Churchill warned that there was still a war to be won in the east.

Instalación de altavoces en Trafalgar Square para el discurso de victoria que pronunciará el rey Jorge VI. El mes de mayo trajo el final de la guerra a Europa, pero Churchill recordó que en el Este aún quedaba una guerra por ganar.

Montaggio di altoparlanti in Trafalgar Square per il discorso della vittoria del re Giorgio VI. Il mese di maggio ha portato la fine della guerra in Europa, ma Churchill ammonisce che c'è ancora una guerra da vincere in Oriente.

Three months later came the big parade. Hundreds of thousands swarm over and around the Victoria Monument in London waiting for the appearance of the Royal family on the balcony of Buckingham Palace, 10 August 1945.

Tres meses después llegó el gran desfile. Cientos de miles de personas rodean el monumento a la reina Victoria, en Londres, esperando que la familia real salga al balcón del Palacio de Buckingham, el 10 de agosto de 1945.

Tre mesi dopo, la grande parata. Centinaia di migliaia di persone circondano il monumento alla regina Vittoria a Londra in attesa dell'apparizione della famiglia reale al balcone di Buckingham Palace, 10 agosto 1945.

It must be true, it's in the paper. A lone GI reads news of the Nazi surrender, 7 May 1945.

Debe de ser verdad lo dice el periódico. Un soldado del GI lee la noticia de la rendición nazi, el 7 de mayo de 1945.

Dev'essere vero, è scritto sul giornale. Un solitario GI legge la notizia della resa nazista, 7 maggio 1945.

Good news travels fast. Jubilant US servicemen prepare to celebrate in New York, 30 April 1945. The end of the war in Europe was only a week away.

Las buenas noticias vuelan. Militares estadounidenses celebran en Nueva York la muerte de Hitler, el 30 de abril de 1945. Quedaba sólo una semana para que terminara la guerra en Europa.

Le buone notizie viaggiano in fretta. Militari americani raggianti si preparano a festeggiare a New York, 30 aprile 1945. Alla fine della guerra in Europa ormai non manca che una settimana.

Children who survived the atom bomb attack on Hiroshima. They are wearing masks to combat the odour of death hanging over the flattened city.

Supervivientes de la explosión de la bomba atómica en Hiroshima. Llevan máscaras para combatir el olor de muerte que invade la ciudad arrasada.

Bambini sopravvissuti alla bomba atomica di Hiroshima. Indossano delle maschere per alleviare l'odore di morte che domina sulla città martire.

6 August 1945.
A mushroom-shaped
cloud marks the
destruction of
Hiroshima, and the
first wartime use of
an atomic bomb.

6 de agosto de 1945.
Una nube en forma
de seta simboliza la
destrucción de
Hiroshima y el
primer lanzamiento
de una bomba
atómica en tiempo
de guerra.

6 agosto 1945.
Una nuvola a forma
di fungo simbolizza
la distruzione di
Hiroshima e il primo
lancio di una bomba
atomica per uso
militare.

The last great age of London street parties, May 1945. Children, mothers, grannies – and a few dads and grandads – pose for the camera at a Victory tea party in Brockley, south-east London. Weeks earlier a V2 flying bomb had killed dozens of children less than a mile away.

Los últimos días de la época dorada de las fiestas callejeras de Londres, en mayo de 1945. Niños y niñas, madres, enfermeras y algunos padres y abuelos posan para la cámara y toman té durante una fiesta de celebración de la victoria, en Brockley, al sureste de Londres. Unas semanas antes, un proyectil V2 había matado a decenas de niños muy cerca de allí.

L'ultima grande epoca delle feste di strada a Londra, maggio 1945. Figli, mamme, nonne – ma pochi papà e nonni – posano per una fotografia alla festa della vittoria a Brockley, nel sud-est di Londra. Poche settimane prima una bomba telecomandata V2 aveva ucciso decine di bambini a poco più di un chilometro da lì.

The 'V' motif gathered momentum towards the end of the war. It had been the call sign for resistance groups in Europe. It had become Churchill's trademark. Here three American soldiers have adopted it as their hairstyle.

La "V" de victoria se puso de moda hacia el final de la guerra. Había sido el símbolo de identidad de los grupos de resistencia de Europa y un gesto típico de Churchill. En la foto, tres soldados estadounidenses la han adoptado como peinado.

La "V" diventa il motivo più alla moda alla fine della guerra. Era il segno di riconoscimento dei gruppi partigiani in Europa e il marchio distintivo di Churchill. Nella foto tre soldati americani l'adottano nel taglio di capelli.

Prague welcomes what many later regarded as a new oppressor. Soviet marshal Ivan Stepanovich Konev arrives with a column of Soviet troops, May 1945. A few months later a British army officer was to write of an 'Iron Curtain across Europe'. Churchill later borrowed the phrase.

Praga da la bienvenida a los que, más tarde, muchos considerarían como los nuevos opresores. El mariscal soviético Ivan Stepanovich Konev entra en la ciudad al frente de una columna de soldados soviéticos, en mayo de 1945. Unos meses después, un oficial del ejército británico escribiría acerca de "un telón de acero que cruza Europa". Más adelante, Churchill tomó prestada la frase y la popularizó.

Praga accoglie coloro che, più tardi, molti avrebbero considerato come i nuovi oppressori. Il maresciallo sovietico Ivan Stepanovich Konev arriva con una colonna di militari sovietici nel maggio 1945. Soltanto pochi mesi dopo un ufficiale britannico avrebbe scritto di una "cortina di ferro abbattutasi sull'Europa". Churchill, in seguito, avrebbe fatto sua questa espressione.

It's all over! Troops and civilians crowd together in
Piccadilly to celebrate the end of the war in Japan,
15 August 1945. There were some who felt relief rather
than elation. And for many the end had come too late.

¡Se terminó! Militares y civiles reunidos en Piccadilly para
celebrar el fin de la guerra en Japón, el 15 de agosto de
1945. Para algunos, el alivio fue mayor que la euforia.
Para muchos, el final había llegado demasiado tarde.

È finita! Militari e civili abbracciati a Piccadilly per
festeggiare la fine della guerra in Giappone, 15 agosto
1945. Alcuni esprimono sollievo più che esaltazione.
E, per molti, la fine della guerra è arrivata troppo tardi.

For the majority,
whether combatants
or civilians, the
end of the fighting
brought a great surge
of joy and hope.

Para la mayoría, ya
fueran combatientes
o civiles, el final de
la guerra trajo una
oleada de alegría y
esperanza.

Per la maggioranza,
soldati o civili che
fossero, la fine delle
ostilità fu un grande
momento di gioia e
speranza.

Rudolf Hess, formerly Hitler's deputy. Hess died in prison 41 years later, having tried to kill himself four times.

Rudolf Hess, la mano derecha de Hitler, murió en prisión 41 años más tarde, tras haber intentado suicidarse en cuatro ocasiones.

Rudolf Hess, l'ex braccio destro di Hitler. Hess morì in prigione 41 anni più tardi, dopo aver tentato di uccidersi quattro volte.

The Nuremberg Trials. Hermann Göring needed only one suicide attempt. He took cyanide just hours before the time fixed for his execution.

Los juicios de Núremberg. Hermann Göring sólo necesitó un intento de suicidio. Tomó una cápsula de cianuro unas horas antes del momento fijado para su ejecución.

Processo di Norimberga. A Hermann Göring è bastato un solo tentativo di suicidio. Masticò una pillola di cianuro alcune ore prima della sua esecuzione.

Two elderly Berliners rest on a bench marked 'Not for Jews', shortly after the end of the war. For them the misery of defeat was not a new experience, but rebuilding their lives would be almost beyond their capabilities.

Dos ancianos berlineses descansan en un banco con la inscripción "Prohibido sentarse a los judíos", poco después del final de la guerra. Para ellos, la tristeza de la derrota no era una experiencia nueva, pero seguramente ya no les quedaban fuerzas para reconstruir sus vidas.

Due vecchi berlinesi si riposano su una panchina dove è scritto: "Vietato sedersi agli ebrei", poco tempo dopo la fine della guerra. Per loro la miseria di una sconfitta militare non è una esperienza nuova, ma ricostruire una nuova vita sarà al di sopra delle loro capacità.

December 1945.
A young orphan
tries to sell his
father's Iron Cross
for the price of a
few cigarettes.

Diciembre de 1945.
Un joven huérfano
intenta vender la
cruz de hierro de
su padre al precio
de un paquete de
cigarrillos.

Dicembre 1945.
Un giovane orfano
tenta di barattare la
croce di ferro del
padre per qualche
sigaretta.

5. Back to normal
Vuelta a la normalidad
Ritorno alla normalità

The immense task that lay ahead, March 1946. Just over a year after
the horrific bombing raid, leading citizens of Dresden plan their
new city: (from left to right) Heinz Grünewald (Propaganda Director),
Walter Weidauer (Mayor), and Dr C Herbert (Town Architect).

Marzo de 1946. Una ingente tarea queda por delante. Apenas un año
después del terrible bombardeo aéreo, eminentes ciudadanos de
Dresde trabajan en la reconstrucción de la ciudad. De izquierda a
derecha: Heiz Grünewald (director de propaganda), Walter Weidauer
(alcalde) y Dr. C. Herbert (arquitecto municipal).

Un lavoro immenso resta da compiere, marzo 1946. Meno di un anno
dopo il terrificante bombardamento aereo, eminenti cittadini di
Dresda programmano la ricostruzione della città: (da sinistra a destra)
Heinz Grünewald (direttore della propaganda), Walter Weidauer
(sindaco) e Dr. C. Herbert (architetto municipale).

5. Back to normal
Vuelta a la normalidad
Ritorno alla normalità

Gas masks were thrown away. Bananas and oranges reappeared. Bomb sites became playgrounds. You still couldn't get all the bread, meat, butter, petrol and clothes that you wanted, but at least your sleep was no longer shattered by the air raid siren at night or the bugler's reveille at daybreak.

In Europe there was a massive shortage of houses. Most German cities lay in ruins. Poland was a wasteland. Large areas of the Netherlands, France, Belgium and Britain had been flattened, though not as horrifically as Hiroshima and Nagasaki. As soon as gas, water and electricity supplies had been restored, however, and the streets cleared of rubble, people began to rebuild their lives and their homes.

It was the era of the spiv and the black marketeer – the shifty guy who could get you eggs, petrol coupons, car tyres, nylon stockings, whatever you wanted – at a price. A few made a fortune. Many came to grief. Most made a precarious living.

The promise was that a brand new world would be created – better hospitals, schools, work conditions, and no more unemployment, no more 'us' and 'them'. It nearly happened. But, somehow, what had seemed so simple as an idea became unattainable in practice.

Todo el mundo se deshizo de las máscaras de gas y en las tiendas reaparecieron los plátanos y las naranjas. Los lugares bombardeados se convirtieron en terrenos de juego. Todavía no podía encontrarse todo el pan, la carne, la mantequilla, el combustible y la ropa que se deseaba, pero al menos el sueño ya no se veía perturbado por las alarmas en plena noche o por el toque de diana al amanecer.

En Europa había una gran falta de viviendas. La mayoría de las ciudades alemanas estaban en ruinas, Polonia era un verdadero desierto y regiones enteras de Holanda, Francia, Bélgica y el Reino Unido habían sido destruidas, aunque no de forma tan terrible como Hiroshima y Nagasaki. Sin embargo, tan pronto como se restablecieron los suministros de agua, gas y electricidad y las calles se limpiaron de escombros, la gente empezó a reconstruir sus casas y sus vidas.

Fue una época de mercado negro y traficantes, de individuos sospechosos que podían conseguir huevos, cupones de carburante, neumáticos, medias de nilón o lo que se quisiera, pero a unos precios desorbitados. Algunos hicieron fortuna, pero para muchos las cosas fueron mal; la mayoría llevaron una vida precaria.

Todas las promesas coincidían en que estaba naciendo un mundo nuevo. Mejores hospitales, escuelas y condiciones laborales, sin desempleo y sin volver a hablar de "nosotros" y "ellos". El sueño casi se hizo realidad, pero lo que parecía tan sencillo en la teoría se convirtió en algo irrealizable en la práctica.

Le maschere a gas vengono buttate via. Ricompaiono le banane e le arance. Le voragini provocate dalle bombe diventano campi da gioco. Non sono ancora disponibili tutto il pane, la carne, il burro, la benzina e i vestiti di cui si avrebbe bisogno, ma almeno non si è più brutalmente svegliati dalle sirene d'allerta dei bombardamenti di notte o dal suono delle trombe all'alba

In Europa si verifica un'impressionante penuria di abitazioni. Gran parte delle città tedesche è distrutta. La Polonia è un deserto. Grandi aree dei Paesi Bassi, Francia, Belgio e Gran Bretagna sono rase al suolo, anche se non così dilaniate come Hiroshima e Nagasaki. Ma quando il gas, l'acqua corrente e l'elettricità vengono riallacciati, la gente comincia a ricostruire la propria vita e le proprie case.

Fu il periodo dei contrabbandieri e del mercato nero: con i maneggioni che potevano procurare uova, buoni per la benzina, pneumatici per le auto, calze di naylon, qualsiasi cosa di cui si avesse bisogno – ma a che prezzo! Alcuni fecero fortuna. Ma per la maggioranza la vita era difficile e quasi tutti vivevano in condizioni di precarietà.

La promessa era la creazione di un mondo completamente nuovo: migliori ospedali, scuole, condizioni di lavoro, fine della disoccupazione, mai più "noi" e "loro". Quasi ci si riuscì. Ma, in realtà, quello che sembrava in teoria molto semplice spesso si rivelò, nella pratica, inattuabile.

A Royal Air Force officer tries on a trilby hat from the limited range of 'demob' (demobilization) issue. Leaving the Forces was like joining up in reverse. Gradually the military personality gave way to a civilian one.

Un oficial de la Royal Air Force se prueba un sombrero de fieltro elegido entre las escasas existencias de la desmovilización. Abandonar el ejército fue como un alistamiento al revés. De una forma gradual, los militares se convirtieron de nuevo en civiles.

Un ufficiale della RAF cerca un cappello tra la limitata scelta che offre un magazzino della "demob" (smobilitazione). Lasciare l'esercito è come un reclutamento al contrario. Poco a poco i militari ridiventano civili.

March 1944. A rehearsal for the real thing. Demobilization was still 18 months away, but already the Allies were confident that the worst of the war was over. A sergeant takes part in a 'demob' practice at an army demobilization centre, Olympia, London.

Marzo de 1944. Un ensayo de la realidad. Faltaban todavía 18 meses para que se iniciara la desmovilización, pero los aliados estaban convencidos de que lo peor de la guerra ya había pasado. Un sargento participa en una prueba en un centro de desmovilización del ejército, en el Olympia de Londres.

Marzo 1944. Una prova per la realtà. La smobilitazione avrebbe avuto luogo 18 mesi più tardi, ma gli alleati già credevano che il peggio della guerra fosse passato. Un sergente prende parte a una prova di smobilitazione in un centro dell'esercito, l'Olympia di Londra.

GI brides leave Southampton, bound for the United States. Before the
war few British women had ever met an American. Now many were
embarking on a new life in a new continent. It was just another example
of the way the war so dramatically changed people's lives.

Novias de soldados norteamericanos abandonan Southampton con
destino a EE.UU. Antes de la guerra eran pocas las mujeres británicas que
conocían a un estadounidense. Ahora, muchas embarcaban hacia una
nueva vida en un nuevo continente. Es sólo otro ejemplo de cómo la
guerra cambió radicalmente la vida de la gente.

Fidanzate di GI lasciano Southampton dirette negli Stati Uniti. Prima della
guerra poche donne britanniche avevano incontrato degli americani.
Adesso parecchie di esse si imbarcano per una nuova vita in un nuovo
continente. Un altro esempio di come la guerra abbia drammaticamente
cambiato la vita di molta gente.

February 1946. A US Marine is reunited with his GI bride and son, newly arrived in the United States. Not all wartime romances ended so happily. There were broken hearts and broken promises all over Europe.

Febrero de 1946. Un marine estadounidense se reúne con su novia e hijo, recién llegados a EE.UU. Pero no todos los romances de la guerra terminaron tan felizmente. En Europa quedaron muchos corazones rotos y promesas incumplidas.

Febbraio 1946. Un soldato della marina americana, appena arrivato negli Stati Uniti, riabbraccia la fidanzata e il figlio. Non tutti i romanzi della guerra ebbero un esito tanto felice. In tutta Europa vi furono cuori infranti e promesse tradite.

August 1946.
A prefabricated
house arrives at its
site. Four lorries
could deliver the
entire house.

Agosto 1946. Una
casa prefabricada
llega a su destino.
Bastaron cuatro
camiones para
trasportar una
vivienda entera.

Agosto 1946. Una
casa prefabbricata
arriva a destinazione.
Quattro camion
erano sufficienti a
trasportare una casa
intera.

Coming back to a new home. Gunner Murdoch arrives at his 'prefab' (prefabricated house) in Tulse Hill, London, to be greeted by his wife and son. He had been away for four and a half years, most of which he had spent as a Japanese prisoner of war.

El regreso a una nueva casa. El artillero Murdoch llega a su casa prefabricada en Tulse Hill, Londres, y su mujer e hijo le dan la bienvenida. Ha estado ausente durante cuatro años y medio y ha pasado casi todo este tiempo como prisionero de guerra japonés.

Tornare in una nuova casa. L'artigliere Murdoch ritorna nella sua nuova casa prefabbricata di Tulse Hill, Londra, dove è accolto dalla moglie e dal figlio. Mancava da casa da quattro anni e mezzo, la maggior parte dei quali li aveva passati come prigioniero in un campo giapponese.

March 1946. A taste of peace. Children sample the
first batch of bananas to arrive in Britain after the
war. Jack Marks, the importer, can just be seen in
the crowd (far right, back).

Marzo de 1946. El sabor de la paz. Un grupo de
niños prueban los primeros plátanos llegados al
Reino Unido después de la guerra. Jack Marks, el
importador, apenas puede verse entre la multitud
(al fondo, derecha).

Marzo 1946. Il gusto della pace. Bambini mangiano
le prime banane arrivate in Gran Bretagna dopo la
guerra. Jack Marks, l'importatore, si intravede
appena tra la folla (a destra, sullo sfondo).

The arrival of such luxuries as bananas was given the same sort of press coverage reserved for film stars or heads of state.

La llegada de lujos tales como los plátanos recibió de la prensa una cobertura reservada a las estrellas de cine y los jefes de Estado.

La notizia dell'arrivo di un prodotto di lusso come le banane veniva data dalla stampa con la stessa enfasi riservata alle star o ai capi di stato.

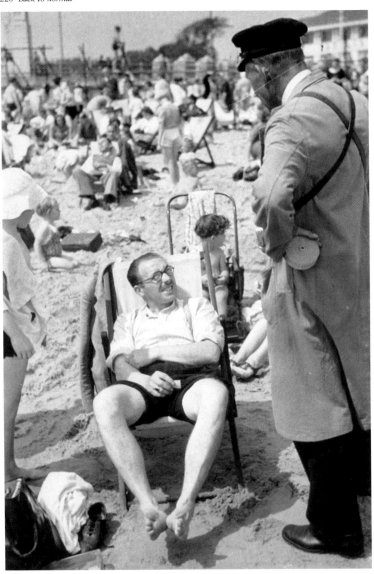

The fight for the
beaches is over, 19
August 1944. This
picture was taken
only two and a half
months after D-day.

La batalla por las
playas ha terminado.
Es el 19 de agosto
de 1944 y esta foto
está tomada sólo dos
meses y medio
después del día D.

La battaglia sulle
spiagge è finita,
19 agosto 1944.
Questa foto è stata
scattata solo due
mesi e mezzo dopo
il D-day.

Most British seaside resorts reopened for business before the war ended, but some beaches were still littered with mines, barbed wire and other relics of the invasion scare. This bather seems determined to brave all that and the awful British weather.

La mayoría de los centros turísticos de la costa británica abrieron antes de que la guerra terminara, aunque algunas playas todavía estaban infestadas de minas, alambradas y otros vestigios de la invasión. Este bañista parece decidido a hacerle frente a todo, incluso al mal tiempo inglés.

La maggior parte delle stazioni balneari della Gran Bretagna riaprirono prima della fine della guerra, ma alcune spiagge erano ancora infestate da mine, filo spinato e altri resti dell'invasione. Questo bagnante sembra determinato a sfidare non solo tutto ciò, ma anche il pessimo clima britannico.

February 1947. Families collect their coke rations
from the South Metropolitan Gas Company's depot at
Vauxhall, London. The winter of 1946/47 was one
of the coldest in memory, and 'back to normal' did not
mean back to plenty. All fuel was still rationed.

Febrero de 1947. Familias recogiendo sus raciones de
carbón en el depósito de la South Metropolitan Gas
Company, en Vauxhall (Londres). El invierno de 1946-
1947 fue uno de los más fríos que se recuerdan, y la
vuelta a la normalidad no significó el retorno a la
abundancia. El carburante todavía estaba racionado.

Febbraio 1947. Alcune famiglie raccolgono la loro
razione di carbone dal deposito della South
Metropolitan Gas Company di Vauxhall, Londra.
L'inverno 1946-47 fu uno dei più freddi a memoria
d'uomo, e il "ritorno alla normalità" non significò il
ritorno all'abbondanza. Tutti i carburanti erano ancora
razionati.

Canadian soldiers of a field hygiene section delouse Russian prisoners of war recently
liberated from a camp near Friesoythe, 30 miles west of Bremen. The Russians had been
prisoners for over two years. They would have been infested with lice for almost all that time.

Soldados canadienses de una sección de higiene de campaña desinfectan a prisioneros de
guerra rusos recientemente liberados de un campo cercano a Friesoythe, a 50 kilómetros de
Bremen. Eran prisioneros desde hacía más de dos años y sin duda habían estado infestados de
pulgas durante todo este tiempo.

In una sezione igienica di campagna, soldati canadesi disinfestano prigionieri russi appena
liberati da un campo vicino Friesoythe, 50 chilometri a ovest di Brema. I russi erano rimasti
prigionieri per più di due anni e, senza dubbio, erano stati tormentati dalle pulci per quasi
tutto il periodo.

April 1948. Nurses
from UNICEF
(United Nations
International
Children's
Emergency Fund)
spray the hair
of a young German
deportee from
Czechoslovakia.
The spray is almost
certainly DDT, and
therefore toxic.

Abril de 1948.
Enfermeras del
UNICEF (Fondo
Internacional de las
Naciones Unidas
para la Ayuda a la
Infancia) pulverizan
los cabellos de una
pequeña alemana
deportada de
Checoslovaquia.
Muy probablemente
le están aplicando
DDT, un producto
tóxico.

Aprile 1948. Alcune
infermiere
dell'UNICEF (Fondo
delle Nazioni Unite
per l'infanzia)
spruzzano i capelli
di una piccola
deportata tedesca
in Cecoslovacchia.
Il prodotto è quasi
certamente DDT
e quindi tossico.

September 1949.
The Berlin airlift
delivers the one
millionth bag of coal
at Gatow Airport,
following the Soviet
Union's blockade of
land routes.

Septiembre de 1949.
El puente aéreo de
Berlín entrega el
saco de carbón
1.000.000 en el
aeropuerto de
Gatow, después de
que la Unión
Soviética bloqueara
los accesos terrestres
a Berlín.

Settembre 1949.
Il ponte aereo di
Berlino porta il
milionesimo pacco
di carbone al Gatow
Airport in seguito al
blocco delle strade
per Berlino imposto
dall'Unione
Sovietica.

A German airlift worker's wife looks after Berlin children as they munch their ration of one slice of bread and margarine. The parcel at the side is from the Red Cross. The Berlin airlift lasted about a year, after the Soviet Union halted all deliveries of food and supplies overland.

La esposa de un trabajador del puente aéreo alemán cuida de un grupo de niños de Berlín mientras toman su ración de pan con mantequilla. El paquete situado sobre la mesa lo ha enviado la Cruz Roja. El puente aéreo de Berlín duró aproximadamente un año, después de que la Unión Soviética prohibiera cualquier suministro de alimentos y víveres por vía terrestre.

Un'ausiliaria tedesca del ponte aereo si cura di alcuni bambini che mangiano la loro razione di cibo: una fetta di pane con margarina. Il pacchetto alla sua destra è della Croce Rossa. Il ponte aereo di Berlino durò circa un anno dopo che l'Unione Sovietica aveva interrotto tutte le consegne di cibo e suppellettili via terra.

The divided city, 1948. This line across Berlin's Potsdamer Straße was to prevent police from the Russian sector pursuing criminals into the Western Zone.

La ciudad dividida, en 1948. Esta línea que atraviesa la Potsdamer Strasse de Berlín era para evitar que la policía del sector ruso persiguiera criminales en la zona occidental.

La città divisa, 1948. Questa linea che attraversa Potsdamer Straße a Berlino, serviva per evitare che la polizia del settore sovietico perseguisse i criminali anche nella zona occidentale.

July 1948.
A displaced person
sells a tin of food to
a Berliner after
hearing that she will
be deported from
the compound at
Mariendorf.

Julio de 1948. Una
refugiada vende una
lata de conserva a
un berlinés tras
saber que deberá
abandonar el campo
de Mariendorf y
regresar a su país.

Luglio 1948. Una
profuga vende una
confezione di
conserva a un
berlinese dopo aver
saputo di essere stata
trasferita a
Mariendorf.

July 1945. Poles await distribution of bread and blankets by UNRRA (United Nations Relief and Rehabilitation Administration) workers at Weimar Station, Germany. The former occupants of a slave labour camp had opted not to return to Poland but to travel west to Bavaria to work on farms.

Julio de 1945. Polacos esperando que miembros de la UNRRA (Agencia de las Naciones Unidas para el Socorro y la Rehabilitación) distribuyan pan y mantas en la estación de Weimar (Alemania). Los antiguos ocupantes de un campo de trabajos forzados decidieron no regresar a Polonia y viajar al oeste hacia Bavaria para buscar trabajo en granjas.

Luglio 1945. Polacchi in attesa della distribuzione di pane e coperte da parte dell'UNRRA (Agenzia delle Nazioni Unite per il soccorso e la riabilitazione), alla stazione di Weimar, in Germania. Costretti precedentemente ai lavori forzati, avevano preferito non ritornare in Polonia e cercare lavoro nelle fattorie della Baviera.

July 1947. A Dutch woman kisses her grandchild for the first time. The barbed wire fence divided the mining town of Kerkrade in two – one half in Germany, the other in the Netherlands. It took years before some families were reunited after the war.

Julio de 1947. Una holandesa besa a su nieto por primera vez. La alambrada dividía en dos partes la ciudad minera de Kerkrade, una quedaba en Alemania y la otra en Holanda. Tras la guerra, hubo que esperar años para que algunas familias volvieran a reunirse.

Luglio 1947. Un'olandese bacia la nipotina per la prima volta. Il filo spinato divideva la città mineraria di Kerkrade in due: metà in Germania e metà in Olanda. Dovettero passare degli anni prima che alcune famiglie riuscissero a riunirsi dopo la guerra.

October 1944. German refugees queue for soup in a former
German army barrack at Brand, near Aachen. The people in the
queue are 'room presidents', each responsible for a section of
refugees. In all, there were 4,500 displaced people in the camp.

Octubre de 1944. Refugiados alemanes hacen cola para recoger
sopa en un antiguo barracón del ejército alemán en Brand, cerca de
Aquisgrán. Las personas de la cola son "presidentes de habitación":
cada una de ellas es el responsable de un grupo de refugiados. En
total, en este campo vivían 4.500 refugiados.

Ottobre 1944. Rifugiati tedeschi in coda per il pranzo in una
baracca che era appartenuta all'esercito tedesco a Brand, vicino
Aquisgrana. La gente in coda è costituita da "rappresentanti di
stanza" ognuno responsabile di un gruppo di rifugiati. I rifugiati nel
campo, in totale, erano 4500.

October 1945.
One of thousands
homeless Germans,
wandering from
East Germany to the
Western Sector
of Berlin, rests for a
while to bathe her
aching feet.

Octubre de 1945.
Uno de los miles de
alemanes sin hogar,
durante su éxodo
desde Alemania
Oriental al sector
occidental de
Berlín, descansa un
momento para lavar
sus piernas doloridas.

Ottobre 1945. Una
delle migliaia di
ragazze senzatetto,
durante l'esodo dalla
Germania dell'Est
verso il settore
occidentale di
Berlino, si riposa un
istante per lavarsi le
gambe doloranti.

May 1945. Frederick Ramage's picture of French, Belgian, Dutch and Polish refugees crossing the Elbe over what is left of the bridge at Tangermünde. The bridge had been blown up by the retreating German army. The refugees are fleeing from the advancing Russians.

Mayo de 1945. Fotografía de Frederick Ramage que muestra a varios refugiados franceses, belgas, holandeses y polacos cruzando el Elba sobre los restos del puente de Tangermünde, destruido por el ejército alemán en su retirada. Los refugiados huyen de los rusos que avanzan hacia ellos.

Maggio 1945. L'immagine di Frederick Ramage rappresenta rifugiati francesi, belgi, olandesi e polacchi che attraversano l'Elba su ciò che resta del ponte di Tangermünde, minato dall'esercito tedesco in ritirata. I rifugiati stanno fuggendo dall'avanzata dell'esercito russo.

Another photograph by Frederick Ramage – July 1945. The streets of Berlin have been cleared of rubble. Public transport has been restored, but there is no room on buses or trams for heavy loads. Women use handcarts to pull what few possessions they have left as they search for somewhere to live.

Otra fotografía de Frederick Ramage, julio de 1945. Las calles de Berlín se han limpiado de escombros. También se ha restablecido el transporte público, pero en los autobuses y tranvías no hay sitio para las cargas pesadas. En la foto, varias mujeres utilizan carretillas para transportar las escasas pertenencias que les quedan mientras buscan algún lugar donde instalarse.

Un'altra fotografia di Frederick Ramage – luglio 1945. Le strade di Berlino sono state ripulite dalle rovine. I trasporti pubblici hanno ricominciato a funzionare, ma non c'è spazio negli autobus o nei tram per i carichi più pesanti. Le donne usano delle carriole per trasporttare i pochi beni che hanno salvato, in cerca di un posto dove vivere.

Two images of postwar Berlin by Frederick Ramage. Soldiers (left) returning from the front and homeless civilians gather at a railway terminus, July 1945. Berlin families (above) pass a Russian poster as they seek a new home, October 1945.

Dos imágenes del Berlín de posguerra, obra de Frederick Ramage. A la izquierda, soldados regresando del frente y civiles sin hogar se hacinan en una estación, en julio de 1945. Arriba, familias berlinesas en busca de un nuevo hogar pasan por delante de un cartel ruso, en octubre de 1945.

Due immagini della Berlino del dopoguerra di Frederick Ramage. A sinistra, soldati di ritorno dal fronte e civili senzatetto riuniti alla stazione ferroviaria, luglio 1945. In alto, famiglie berlinesi alla ricerca di una nuova casa passano davanti a un manifesto sovietico, ottobre 1945.

1949. Groundnuts
(peanuts) from East
Africa, grown in a
government-
sponsored initiative,
are sucked from
the hold of a cargo
ship in the London
Docks.

1949. Cacahuetes
de África Oriental,
fruto de una
iniciativa financiada
por el gobierno, son
aspirados de la
bodega de un buque
de carga en los
muelles de Londres.

1949. Noccioline
provenienti
dall'Africa orientale,
raccolte su iniziativa
del governo, sono
risucchiate dalla
stiva di un cargo nei
docks di Londra.

February 1949. The 'European Recovery Program', known as Marshall Aid, brings sugar to the Royal Victoria Docks, London. The scheme began in 1947.

Febrero de 1949. Descarga de azúcar caribeño en los muelles Royal Victoria de Londres, dentro del "European Recovery Program", también conocido como Plan Marshall, que se inició en 1947.

Febbraio 1949. L'"European Recovery Program", più conosciuto come piano Marshall, consegna lo zucchero ai Royal Victoria Docks di Londra. Il progetto iniziò nel 1947.

January 1947. Two limbless ex-servicemen make artificial limbs
for others maimed by the war. They were taking part in an
exhibition sponsored by the Ministries of Health and Labour.

Enero de 1947. Dos antiguos soldados que perdieron un
antebrazo fabrican antebrazos ortopédicos para otros mutilados
de guerra. Participan en una exposición organizada por los
ministerios de salud y trabajo.

Gennaio 1947. Due ex soldati privi di un braccio fabbricano
braccia artificiali per altri invalidi di guerra. Partecipano a
una esposizione organizzata dal ministero della sanità e del
lavoro.

German production lines roll again, 1947. This is the final operation on the assembly line of a Ford factory. The United States pumped vast economic aid into Germany after the war to prevent Communism creeping ever westwards.

En 1947 las cadenas de producción alemanas se ponen de nuevo en funcionamiento. En la foto, las operaciones finales en la cadena de montaje de una fábrica de la Ford. EE.UU. brindó a Alemania una importante ayuda económica después de la guerra para impedir que el comunismo avanzara hacia el oeste.

La produzione tedesca ricomincia a funzionare, 1947. Nella foto le ultime operazioni alla catena di montaggio di una fabbrica Ford. Dopo la guerra gli Stati Uniti avevano fornito un considerevole aiuto economico alla Germania per impedire che il comunismo si propagasse ulteriormente in Occidente.

Bricklayers working for the Ilford Borough Council, July 1947. 'Homes fit for heroes' had been a slogan and a broken promise after World War I. The Labour Government did more to house people decently after World War II.

Albañiles trabajando para el Ilford Borough Council, en julio de 1947. "Hogares para los héroes", un eslogan difundido tras la Primera Guerra Mundial, se convirtió en una promesa incumplida. Después de la Segunda Guerra Mundial, el gobierno laborista realizó un mayor esfuerzo para que la gente tuviera un hogar decente.

Muratori al lavoro per l'Ilford Borough Council, luglio 1947. "Case per gli eroi" era stato lo slogan, in realtà una promessa mai mantenuta, dopo la prima guerra mondiale. Il governo laburista fece di più per fornire case decenti alla gente dopo la seconda guerra mondiale.

Dresden, March 1946. Gustav and Alma Piltz help to clear rubble just over a year after the RAF and the USAF reduced their city to a smoking ruin. Two generations later the Allied raids on Dresden are still the subject of much controversy.

Dresde, en marzo de 1946. Gustav y Alma Piltz ayudan a retirar escombros apenas un año después de que la RAF y la USAF convirtieran su ciudad en un montón de ruinas humeantes. Dos generaciones más tarde, los ataques aéreos de los aliados sobre Dresde son todavía fuente de controversia.

Dresda, marzo 1946. Gustav e Alma Piltz aiutano a eliminare le macerie poco meno di un anno dopo che la RAF e l'aviazione militare USA avevano ridotto la città in una rovina fumante. Due generazioni dopo, i bombardamenti degli alleati su Dresda sono ancora oggetto di numerose controversie.

Dresden, March 1946. A human chain of women workers move bricks to be used in the rebuilding of their city. In the background are the remains of the Roman Catholic cathedral. Until the Allied raid, Dresden had been one of the Baroque centres of beauty in Europe.

Dresde, en marzo de 1946. Una cadena humana de mujeres trasladan ladrillos para reconstruir la ciudad. Al fondo se ven los restos de la catedral católica. Dresde había sido una de las ciudades barrocas más bellas de Europa hasta los ataques aéreos aliados.

Dresda, marzo 1946. Una catena umana di lavoratrici trasporta i mattoni per la ricostruzione della città. Sullo sfondo si stagliano i resti della cattedrale cattolica. Prima dei bombardamenti Dresda era una delle più belle città barocche d'Europa.

In their first summer of peace since 1939, citizens of Magdeburg queue for water at a pump. It is a scene that could have been witnessed in almost any German city in 1945.

En su primer verano de paz desde 1939, ciudadanos de Magdeburgo hacen cola para obtener agua de un pozo. En 1945, esta escena podía verse en casi todas las ciudades de Alemania.

Durante la prima estate di pace dal 1939, alcuni cittadini di Magdeburgo fanno la fila davanti a una pompa d'acqua. Questa scena si sarebbe potuta vedere praticamente in quasi tutte le città tedesche.

Just a few months after the beginning of
the Marshall Aid programme, German
women water young trees in a horticultural
nursery.

Mujeres alemanas riegan árboles jóvenes en
un vivero, pocos meses después de iniciarse
el Plan Marshall.

Appena pochi mesi dopo l'inizio del piano
Marshall, alcune donne tedesche innaffiano
i giovani arbusti di un vivaio ortofrutticolo.

Berliner Straße in the Western Sector of the city, 1948. Self-help complements Marshall Aid from the USA. The worst of the suffering was over. A year or two earlier these street allotments would have been ravaged by starving refugees.

La Berliner Straße, en el sector occidental de la ciudad, en 1948. La autosubsistencia complementó las ayudas del Plan Marshall estadounidense. Lo peor ya había pasado. Uno o dos años antes, estos huertos callejeros hubieran sido tomados por los hambrientos refugiados.

La Berliner Straße nel settore occidentale della città nel 1948. Le iniziative individuali si aggiungono al piano Marshall americano. Il peggio è passato. Uno o due anni prima questi orti per strada sarebbero stati presi d'assalto da profughi affamati.

November 1948. A Berlin park has become a wilderness. For the young, there is nowhere to play. For the elderly, there is nowhere to sit. The wood from the park benches has been torn off and taken away to be used for fuel.

Noviembre de 1948. Un parque de Berlín en total abandono. Para los pequeños no hay ningún sitio para jugar. Para los mayores, ningún lugar para sentarse. La madera de los bancos se ha arrancado para utilizarla como combustible.

Novembre 1948. Un parco berlinese abbandonato. Per i bambini non c'è un posto dove giocare. Per i vecchi non c'è posto per sedere. La legna delle panchine è stata divelta e usata come combustibile.

July 1945. An old
woman clears rubble
in the Russian Zone
of Berlin (picture by
Frederick Ramage).

Julio de 1945.
Una mujer limpia
escombros en el
sector ruso de Berlín
(foto de Frederik
Ramage).

Luglio 1945.
Un'anziana donna
rimuove le macerie
nella zona russa
di Berlino (foto di
Frederick Ramage).

6. New nations, new problems
Nuevas naciones, nuevos problemas
Nuove nazioni, nuovi problemi

The homeless come home, the wanderers come to rest. Jewish refugees arrive at a British camp on their way to Palestine in 1947, a year in which Zionist terrorism was at its height and an independent Israel still seemed heartbreaks away.

Las personas sin hogar regresan a casa. Multitudes de nómadas por fin pueden descansar. En la foto, refugiados judíos llegan a un campo de acogida británico en su viaje hacia Palestina en 1947, un año en el que el terrorismo sionista alcanzó máximos y un Israel independiente todavía parecía una utopía.

I senzatetto trovano casa, gli sfollati un luogo dove sostare. Nella foto, profughi ebrei rifugiati arrivano in un campo britannico nel loro viaggio verso la Palestina nel 1947, un anno in cui il terrorismo sionista è al suo apice e un Israele indipendente sembra soltanto un'utopia.

6. New nations, new problems
Nuevas naciones, nuevos problemas
Nuove nazioni, nuovi problemi

By the late summer of 1945 millions of bewildered and homeless people were on the move – across Europe and the Far East. They were looking for somewhere to live, and for many of them that meant a new country.

It was a time of change. The old European colonial powers were bankrupt. Imperial futures had been mortgaged to the hilt to raise money for the war. And, to ensure the cooperation of their subjects, the old rulers had made promises that were now being called in. India demanded independence. Muslims in that subcontinent demanded partition. Jews demanded a land of their own. In China, no demand was necessary. The Communists simply took over.

In all these places there was more killing. In its first year, the new state of Israel had to survive a war against five Arab neighbours. But the actual process was sometimes surprisingly easy. Britain left India with scarcely a murmur.

Where possible, the newly established United Nations did what it could to help, establishing camps for refugees, trying to reunite families that had been blown apart by the misfortunes of war. It was a slow and heartbreaking task.

A finales del verano de 1945, millones de personas desplazadas y sin hogar deambulaban por Europa y Extremo Oriente en busca de algún lugar para vivir, lo que para muchos significó establecerse en otro país.

Fue una época de cambios. Las antiguas potencias coloniales europeas estaban en quiebra. El esperanzador futuro se veía ahora completamente hipotecado debido a la necesidad de obtener fondos para la guerra. Además, para asegurar la cooperación de los ciudadanos, los viejos gobernantes hicieron promesas que ahora se les exigía que mantuvieran. India reclamaba la independencia, mientras que los musulmanes de ese subcontinente pedían la división; los judíos querían una tierra propia y en China no era necesario realizar demanda alguna, pues los comunistas simplemente se hicieron con el poder.

En todos estos lugares se continuaba matando. Durante su primer año de vida, el nuevo Estado de Israel tuvo que hacer frente a una guerra contra cinco vecinos árabes. Pero a veces todo resultaba sorprendentemente fácil. Así, el Reino Unido concedió la independencia a India sin apenas oponer resistencia.

Allá donde fuera posible, la Organización de las Naciones Unidas, creada recientemente, hacía todo lo que estaba en sus manos para ayudar, construyendo campos para los refugiados e intentando reunir a las familias separadas por los avatares de la guerra. Fue una tarea lenta y agotadora.

Alla fine dell'estate del 1945 milioni di uomini senza più domicilio erano in movimento attraverso l'Europa e l'Estremo Oriente. Erano alla ricerca di un luogo dove vivere, e in molti casi adirittura, di un nuovo paese.

Fu un'epoca di cambiamenti. Le vecchie potenze coloniali erano alla bancarrotta. Il futuro degli imperi era stato ipotecato per il bisogno di denaro durante la guerra. E per garantire la cooperazione dei loro sudditi, i vecchi governatori avevano fatto promesse che adesso dovevano mantenere. L'India reclamava l'indipendenza. I musulmani del subcontinente pretendevano la divisione. Gli ebrei volevano una patria che gli appartenesse interamente. In Cina non fu necessaria alcuna richiesta. I comunisti semplicemente presero il potere.

In queste zone si continuava a uccidere. Nel primo anno, il nuovo stato d'Israele dovette sopportare una guerra contro i vicini arabi. Ma, in realtà, il processo fu talvolta sorprendentemente facile. Senza troppo rumore, la Gran Bretagna restituì la libertà all'India.

Dov'era possibile le Nazioni Unite, recentemente create, facevano il possibile per aiutare, istituire campi profughi, cercare di riunire famiglie che erano state divise dalle circostanze avverse. Fu una sfida lunga e faticosa.

22 July 1946.
Ninety-one people
died when the King
David Hotel in
Jerusalem was blown
up by Zionists.

22 de julio de 1946.
Noventa y nueve
personas murieron
en un atentado
sionista contra el
hotel King David
de Jerusalén.

22 luglio 1946.
91 persone muoiono
per una bomba
piazzata dai sionisti
all'hotel King David
di Gerusalemme.

Bandages and bullets. A Jewish doctor tends a wounded man, while his comrade takes aim. The setting is the strife-ridden area of Palestine between Jewish Tel Aviv and the Arab city of Jaffa. The state of Israel was born in war, and spent its youth fighting for survival.

Vendas y balas. Un médico judío atiende a una herida, mientras un soldado apunta con el fusil. La escena tiene lugar en una zona de conflicto de Palestina entre el Tel Aviv judío y la ciudad árabe de Jaffa. El Estado de Israel nació en guerra y pasó su juventud luchando por sobrevivir.

Bende e proiettili. Un medico ebreo soccorre un ferito mentre un soldato prende la mira. La scena si svolge nella zona di conflitto tra Tel Aviv e la città araba di Jaffa, in Palestina. Lo stato di Israele nasce nella guerra e cresce tra i combattimenti per la poropria sopravvivenza.

An exodus that failed: British troops guard a trainload of Jews in Hamburg docks, 1947. The Jews on board had hoped to sail to Palestine in the first 'exodus' ship, *Ocean Vigour*. Instead, they were rounded up, to be sent to the Poppendorf Camp.

Un éxodo que fracasó: soldados británicos vigilan un tren de judíos en los muelles de Hamburgo, en 1947. Los pasajeros de este tren esperaban regresar a Palestina en el primer barco del "éxodo", el *Ocean Vigour*. En vez de ello, fueron enviados al campo de Poppendorf.

Un esodo fallito: soldati britannici sorvegliano un treno carico di ebrei nei docks di Amburgo nel 1947. Gli ebrei sul treno speravano di raggiungere la Palestina sulla prima nave dell'"esodo", la *Ocean Vigour*. Furono invece inviati al campo di Poppendorf.

One of the ringleaders of the 'exodus' movement is placed under arrest, to be taken under close guard to the camp. Coming so soon after the Holocaust, these traumatic echoes of Auschwitz and Buchenwald inflamed Zionist feelings.

Uno de los líderes del "éxodo" es arrestado y llevado a un campo de refugiados. Ecos de las traumáticas experiencias de Auschwitz y Buchenwald, acaecidos tan poco tiempo después del Holocausto, inflamaron los sentimientos sionistas.

Uno dei fomentatori dell'"exodus" è messo sotto arresto e scortato in un campo. Questi echi di Auschwitz e Buchenwald a così poca distanza dall'Olocausto infiammavano gli animi dei sionisti.

An exodus that succeeded: Jewish refugees struggle ashore from the SS *United States*, February 1948. The ship beached near Haifa, after evading British patrol boats on the voyage from Bari, Italy. On board were 700 Jews from Central Europe.

Un éxodo que terminó con éxito: refugiados judíos del SS *United States* intentan llegar a la orilla, en febrero de 1948. El barco partió de Bari, en Italia, y amarró cerca de Haifa, tras evitar a las patrullas costeras británicas. A bordo viajaban 700 judíos procedentes de Europa central.

Un esodo riuscito: rifugiati ebrei raggiungono la riva dalla nave SS *United States*, febbraio 1948. La nave era salpata da Bari e aveva attraccato vicino Haifa dopo avere eluso il controllo navale britannico. Portava a bordo 700 profughi ebrei originari in prevalenza dell'Europa centrale.

Jewish refugees on their way to Palestine, 1945, photographed by Erich Auerbach. On many of the refugee ships, the conditions were appalling – overcrowded, lacking food and water, no knowledge of how long the journey would take, and always the fear that the ship would be intercepted.

Refugiados judíos con destino a Palestina, en 1945, fotografiados por Erich Auerbach. A menudo las condiciones del viaje eran pésimas: barcos sobrecargados, sin agua ni alimentos, sin la menor idea de cuánto duraría el viaje y con la amenaza de ser interceptados en cualquier momento.

Rifugiati ebrei in viaggio verso la Palestina nel 1945 in una fotografia di Erich Auerbach. Le condizioni di viaggio erano spesso drammatiche: imbarcazioni sovraffollate, scarsità d'acqua e cibo, insicurezza sulla durata del viaggio, e sempre la paura che la nave venisse intercettata.

British troops question a young Jewish refugee on her arrival at Haifa in 1945. Within weeks of the end of the war the exodus began.

Soldados británicos interrogan a una joven judía refugiada a su llegada a Haifa en 1945. El éxodo empezó pocas semanas después de que terminara la guerra.

Soldati britannici interrogano una giovane rifugiata ebrea al suo arrivo a Haifa nel 1945. L'esodo ebbe inizio poche settimane dopo la fine della guerra.

Calcutta, August 1946. Rioting flared between Hindus and Muslims when the British announced their plans to withdraw from the Indian subcontinent, and to create the separate states of India and Pakistan.

Calcuta, agosto de 1946. El conflicto entre hindúes y musulmanes estalló cuando los británicos anunciaron su intención de retirarse del subcontinente indio y crear dos estados separados, India y Paquistán.

Calcutta, agosto 1946. Quando la Gran Bretagna annuncia il suo ritiro dal subcontinente indiano e l'intenzione di creare due stati, l'India e il Pakistan, scoppiano violenti scontri tra le comunità indù e musulmana.

Calcutta police use tear gas to clear the streets. Over 2,000 people were killed in the riots, and 4,000 injured. At this stage it was feared that partition would lead inevitably to civil war.

La policía de Calcuta utiliza gases lacrimógenos contra los manifestantes. Más de 2.000 personas murieron en los disturbios callejeros y más de 4.000 resultaron heridas. En ese momento se temía que la división en dos estados llevaría inevitablemente a la guerra civil.

La polizia di Calcutta utilizza gas lacrimogeni per reprimere una manifestazione. Più di 2000 persone furono uccise e 4000 ferite durante gli scontri. In questa fase si temeva che la divisione avrebbe inevitabilmente condotto alla guerra civile.

July 1945. Indian leader Jawaharlal Nehru addresses a huge crowd from the balcony of his house in Simla. The movement for Indian independence had gained strength during the war, many Indians refusing to fight on the British side.

Julio de 1945. El líder indio Jawaharlal Nehru se dirige a la multitud desde el balcón de su casa en Simla. El movimiento para la independencia de India se afianzó durante la guerra y muchos indios se negaron a luchar al lado de los británicos.

Luglio 1945. Il leader indiano Jawaharlal Nehru parla a una folla immensa dal balcone di casa sua a Simla. Il movimento per l'indipendenza indiana si rinforzò durante la guerra e molti indiani si rifiutarono di combattere al fianco dei britannici.

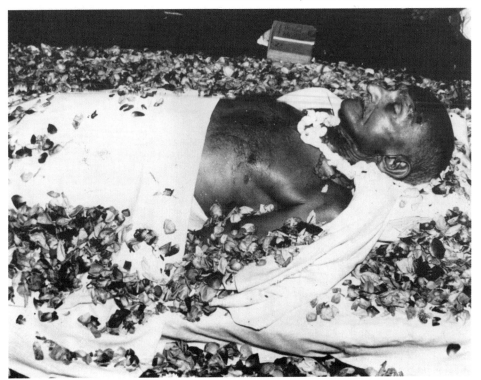

2 February 1948. The body of Mohandas Gandhi lies in state at Birla House, New Delhi. His Hindu assassin opposed Gandhi's policy of communal and religious tolerance. 'The light has gone out of our lives and there is darkness everywhere,' mourned prime minister Nehru.

2 de febrero de 1948. El cuerpo de Mohandas Gandhi, expuesto en Birla House, en Nueva Delhi. Su asesino hindú se oponía a la política de tolerancia política y religiosa promulgada por Gandhi. "La luz ha desaparecido de nuestras vidas y la oscuridad lo ha invadido todo", declaró con tristeza el primer ministro Nehru.

2 febbraio 1948. La salma del Mahatma Gandhi viene esposta alla Birla House, a Nuova Delhi. Il suo assassino indù si opponeva alla politica di Gandhi di tolleranza politica e religiosa. "La luce si è spenta nelle nostre vite e ovunque regnano le tenebre" dichiarò il primo ministro Nehru.

Bombay, 21 August 1947. When partition finally came, it was greeted with huge joy by Hindus and Muslims alike, though Gandhi himself took little part in the celebrations. He was in Calcutta, trying to calm both Hindus and Muslims.

Bombay, el 21 de agosto de 1947. Cuando la división se hizo finalmente realidad, tanto hindúes como musulmanes la recibieron con gran alegría, aunque Gandhi apenas participó en las celebraciones. Se encontraba en Calcuta, intentando calmar a hindúes y musulmanes.

Bombay, 21 agosto 1947. Quando la divisione fu finalmente proclamata fu salutata con immensa gioia tanto dai musulmani quanto dagli indù, anche se lo stesso Gandhi partecipò poco alle celebrazioni. Si trovava a Calcutta, cercando di calmare indù e musulmani.

Karachi, 22 August 1947.
Muslim crowds attend Id prayers
at the mosque.

Karachi, el 22 de agosto de
1947. Una impresionante
multitud de musulmanes realizan
sus plegarias en la mezquita.

Karachi, 22 agosto 1947. Una
folla di musulmani si prostra
durante la preghiera nella
moschea.

Last years of the Raj, 1945. Earl Wavell, Viceroy of India (in pith helmet) watches Indian children eating at the Rotary Club free kitchen in south Calcutta. Wavell was succeeded by Lord Louis Mountbatten in March 1947.

Los últimos años del Raj, el dominio británico sobre India, en 1945. El conde Wavell, virrey de India (con un casco colonial), observa un grupo de niños indios que están comiendo en la cocina al aire libre del Rotary Club, al sur de Calcuta. A Wavell le sucedió lord Louis Mountbatten en marzo de 1947.

Gli ultimi anni del Raj, nel 1945. Il conte Wavell, viceré delle Indie (con il casco coloniale) osserva alcuni bambini indiani mentre mangiano nella cucina all'aperto del Rotary Club a sud di Calcutta. A Wavell succedette Lord Louis Mountbatten, nel marzo 1947.

Last days of the Raj,
August 1947.
Viceroy Lord
Mountbatten and his
wife are surrounded
by children in
New Delhi, only
days before Indian
independence.

Los últimos días del
Raj, el dominio
británico sobre
India, en agosto de
1947. El virrey lord
Mountbatten y su
esposa, rodeados de
niños y niñas en
Nueva Delhi, tan
sólo unos días antes
de la independencia
de India.

Gli ultimi giorni del
Raj, agosto 1947.
Il viceré Lord
Mountbatten e la
moglie vengono
circondati da alcuni
ragazzi a Nuova
Dehli, proprio pochi
giorni prima
dell'indipendenza
indiana.

Brave newcomers to an old world, 1948. Recently arrived Jamaican immigrants in London study a map of the Underground. Large numbers of West Indians arrived after the war in response to invitations from UK-based companies.

Recién llegados a un viejo mundo, 1948. Inmigrantes jamaicanos que acaban de llegar a Londres consultan un mapa del metro. Un gran número de caribeños se trasladaron al Reino Unido después de la guerra en respuesta a las invitaciones realizadas por varias empresas de este país.

Nuovi arrivi nel vecchio mondo, 1948. Immigrati giamaicani, recentemente arrivati a Londra, studiano una mappa della metropolitana. Un gran numero di abitanti caraibici erano arrivati dopo la guerra attirati da società che avevano la loro sede in Gran Bretagna.

July 1949. A newly
arrived West Indian
immigrant looks
for lodgings in
Liverpool. They may
not be easy to find.

Julio de 1949. Un
inmigrante recién
llegado del Caribe
busca alojamiento en
Liverpool, una tarea
sin duda nada fácil.

Luglio 1949.
Un emigrante appena
giunto dai Caraibi
cerca casa a
Liverpool. Non sarà
tanto facile trovarla.

Brave newcomers to a new world, 1940. Nobel laureate
Albert Einstein and his wife Margot take the oath of allegiance
to become citizens of the United States. Einstein's secretary,
Rene Dakas, is on the extreme left.

Recién llegados a un mundo nuevo, 1940. El premio Nobel
Albert Einstein y su esposa Margot prestan el juramento de
lealtad para convertirse en ciudadanos de EE.UU. La secretaria
de Einstein, Rene Dakas, aparece a la izquierda de la foto.

Nuovi arrivi nel nuovo mondo, 1940. Il premio Nobel, Albert
Einstein e la moglie Margot prestano il giuramento di fedeltà
per diventare cittadini degli Stati Uniti. La segretaria di Einstein,
Rene Dakas, è all'estrema sinistra.

The slow lane, August 1940. Immigrants crowd Brooklyn Post Office to register for US citizenship. They have four months to complete the process. Each one will be fingerprinted and screened before admission to 'the greatest democracy in the world'.

Una larga cola de espera, en agosto de 1940. La oficina de correos de Brooklyn, colapsada por inmigrantes que solicitan la nacionalidad estadounidense. Tienen cuatro meses para completar el proceso. A cada uno de ellos se le tomarán las huellas dactilares y se le interrogará antes de ser admitido en "la mayor democracia del mundo".

Lunga fila d'attesa, agosto 1940. Una folla di emigranti all'ufficio postale di Brooklyn in attesa della registrazione per ottenere la nazionalità americana. Le procedure duravano quattro mesi. A ognuno venivano prese le impronte digitali e tutti venivano interrogati prima di entrare nella "più grande democrazia del mondo".

January 1946. An UNRRA official checks the nationalities of arrivals at a displaced persons' camp near Germany.

Enero de 1946. Una funcionaria de la UNRRA comprueba las nacionalidades de las personas que entran en un campo para desplazados situado cerca de Alemania.

Gennaio 1946. Un funzionario dell'UNRRA verifica la nazionalità degli arrivati in un campo profughi vicino alla Germania.

January 1946.
Men of the Royal
Artillery check the
countries sending
delegates to the
first UN conference
in London.

Enero de 1946.
Miembros de la
Royal Artillery
revisan los países
que envían
delegados a la
primera conferencia
de la ONU en
Londres.

Gennaio 1946.
Uomini della
artiglieria reale
controllano quali
paesi hanno
mandato delegati
alla prima
conferenza
dell'ONU a Londra.

7. Showbusiness
El mundo del espectáculo
Lo show-business

'Don't sit under the apple tree with anyone else
but me, till I come marching home...' The
close harmony serenading of the Andrews Sisters
was the epitome of the sound of the Forties.

"No te sientes debajo del manzano con otro,
hasta el día que yo vuelva..." Esta íntima
melodía de las Andrews Sisters era la canción
típica de los años cuarenta.

"Non stare sotto il melo con nessun altro che
me, finché a casa non ritorno..." L'orecchiabile
serenata delle Andrews Sisters è la tipica canzone
degli anni Quaranta.

7. Showbusiness
El mundo del espectáculo
Lo show-business

There were those who believed that Hollywood won the war. It wasn't just a matter of Errol Flynn capturing Burma single-handed, or Walter Pigeon rescuing the British Expeditionary Force from Dunkirk. Hollywood thrust its stars into selling war bonds, entertaining troops, running the stage door canteen, keeping alive the American Dream. Films ran off the production line like tanks or planes. The studio system was at its best and busiest. Radio audiences numbered tens of millions. In Britain the aural gems included Tommy Handley's *ITMA*, *Workers' Playtime*, and the new *Desert Island Discs* series. In the United States there was *The Jack Benny Show*, *The Bing Crosby Show* and *Burns and Allen*. Of the non-professional broadcasters, only Churchill and the British Nazi propagandist 'Lord Haw-Haw' achieved comparable fame.

While the war lasted, dancers, actors, musicians and entertainers signed up for ENSA – officially 'Entertainments National Service Association', sarcastically 'Every Night Something Awful'. They performed in factories and improvised theatres, on the backs of lorries, in aircraft hangars, even on the decks of ships. The quality varied, the response was always enthusiastic.

And for those who performed in night clubs, there were still enough customers to keep the Scotch flowing, if not the champagne.

Algunos afirmaban que fue Hollywood quien ganó la guerra. Y no solo porque Errol Flynn conquistara Birmania con una sola mano o Walter Pigeon rescatara al cuerpo de expedicionarios británico en Dunquerque, sino, sobre todo, porque Hollywood envió a Europa sus estrellas como propaganda de guerra, para entretener a las tropas y servir en las cantinas, en definitiva, para mantener vivo el sueño americano. La industria cinematográfica, que pasó por uno de sus mejores momentos durante la contienda, producía películas como si de tanques o aviones se tratara. Las audiencias radiofónicas se contaban por decenas de millones de personas. En el Reino Unido, las emisiones más populares eran *ITMA* de Tommy Handley, *Worker's Playtime* y la nueva serie *Desert Island Discs*. En EE.UU. hacían furor *The Jack Benny Show*, *The Bing Crosby Show* y *Burns and Allen*. Entre los que no eran profesionales de la radio, sólo Churchill y el propagandista nazi británico lord Haw-Haw alcanzaron una popularidad comparable.

Mientras duró la guerra, bailarines, actores, músicos y todo tipo de artistas actuaban para el ENSA, que oficialmente significaba "Entertainers National Service Association" (asociación del servicio nacional de artistas), pero que recibió irónicamente el sobrenombre de "Every Night Something Awful" (cada noche algo malísimo). Actuaban en fábricas y teatros improvisados, utilizando camiones como escenario, en hangares de aviones e incluso en cubiertas de barcos. La calidad de las funciones era más bien irregular, pero la respuesta del público era siempre entusiasta.

Los que actuaban en clubes nocturnos tenían la suerte de que siempre había suficientes clientes para que durante toda la noche corriera el whisky y, algunas veces, el champaña.

C'era chi credeva che a vincere la guerra fosse stata Hollywood. Non tanto per l'immagine di Errol Flynn che conquista la Birmania con un colpo di mano, o di Walter Pigeon che salva il Corpo di spedizione britannico a Dunquerque. Hollywood coinvolge le sue star nella vendita di buoni di guerra, nell'intrattenimento delle truppe, nell'allietare le mense, nel tenere vivo il sogno americano. Gli ascoltatori della radio si contavano a milioni. In Gran Bretagna le trasmissioni più popolari erano l'*ITMA* di Tommy Handley, *Workers' Playtime* e la nuova serie dei *Desert Island Discs*. Negli Stati Uniti c'erano *The Jack Benny Show*, *The Bing Crosby Show* e *Burns and Allen*. Tra i non professionisti soltanto Churchill e il propagandista filonazista britannico "Lord Haw-Haw" acquistarono una fama paragonabile alla loro.

Per tutta la durata della guerra ballerini, attori, musicisti e presentatori prestarono servizio per l'ENSA, l'"Entertainments National Service Association", ribattezzata ironicamente "Every Night Something Awful". Recitavano nelle fabbriche o in teatri improvvisati, sulle piattaforme dei camion, negli hangar degli aeroporti, persino sui ponti delle navi. La qualità poteva variare ma la risposta era sempre entusiastica. E per coloro che si esibivano nei night club, c'erano sempre abbastanza consumatori per far scorrere il whisky, se non addirittura lo champagne.

Hollywood stars in the real world. Colonel James Stewart returns to America
on the troopship *Queen Elizabeth* after a tour of duty in Europe (above). Captain Clark
Gable at work with the guns of a Flying Fortress (right).

Las estrellas de Hollywood se acercan a la realidad. El coronel James Stewart vuelve a
América en el *Queen Elizabeth* después de una gira de servicio por Europa (superior). El
capitán Clark Gable apunta con una ametralladora en una fortaleza volante (derecha).

Star di Hollywood nel mondo reale. Il colonnello James Stewart rientra in America sulla
nave per il trasporto delle truppe *Queen Elizabeth* dopo una tournée tenuta in Europa
(in alto). Il capitano Clark Gable alla mitragliatrice su una fortezza volante (a destra).

British and Hollywood film star David Niven in the role of compère
for a concert given by Glenn Miller and the Band of the AEF
in London, 1944. Niven was an army officer throughout the war.

El británico David Niven, estrella del cine de Hollywood, encargado
de los acompañamientos en un concierto de Glenn Miller y su
orquesta en el AEF, en Londres, en 1944. Niven fue oficial del
ejército durante la guerra.

David Niven, vedette del cinema britannico e hollywoodiano, nel
ruolo di ospite per un concerto di Glenn Miller e la sua orchestra
all'AEF di Londra, 1944. Niven fu ufficiale dell'esercito durante
tutta la guerra.

The most famous band of World War II: Glenn Miller at work in a London club. Later that year, while flying to France, Miller's plane disappeared. His death is still a mystery.

La orquesta más famosa de la Segunda Guerra Mundial: Glenn Miller dirigiendo a sus músicos en un club de Londres. En ese mismo año, el avión de Glenn Miller desapareció mientras volaba hacia Francia. Las causas de su muerte son todavía un misterio.

L'orchestra più celebre della seconda guerra mondiale: Glenn Miller in un club di Londra. Nello stesso anno l'aereo che lo stava portando in Francia scomparve. La sua morte resta tuttora un mistero.

GIs cluster round Marlene Dietrich, 'somewhere in France', 1945. Dietrich
was born in Berlin, but left for Hollywood in 1930. Hitler ordered her back
to Germany, but she refused, and became an Allied idol during the war.

Soldados del GI rodean a Marlene Dietrich, en algún lugar de Francia, en
1945. Dietrich había nacido en Berlín, pero se trasladó a Hollywood en
1930. Hitler le pidió que regresara a Alemania, pero ella rechazó la
invitación y se convirtió en un ídolo para los aliados durante la guerra.

Alcuni GI circondano Marlene Dietrich "da qualche parte in Francia",
1945. Marlene Dietrich era nata a Berlino, ma si trasferì a Hollywood
nel 1930. Hitler le ordinò di ritornare in Germania, ma si rifiutò
diventando, durante la guerra, uno degli idoli degli alleati.

Hudson River, August 1945. Marlene Dietrich's million-dollar legs are seen hovering over the water on her return to the United States on the *Queen Elizabeth* after entertaining the troops in Europe.

El río Hudson, en agosto de 1945. Marlene Dietrich exhibe sus legendarias piernas a bordo del *Queen Elizabeth,* de regreso a EE.UU., después de haber entretenido a las tropas norteamericanas en Europa.

Hudson River, agosto 1945. Marlene Dietrich esibisce le sue gambe leggendarie mentre si libra sull'acqua al suo ritorno negli Stati Uniti a bordo della *Queen Elizabeth,* dopo avere intrattenuto le truppe americane in Europa.

Dancers at the Windmill Theatre in London rehearse in gas masks and tin hats. Apart from a compulsory closure for two weeks in September 1939, the Windmill was the only London theatre that stayed open throughout the war. For years afterwards, it proudly boasted, 'We never closed.'

Bailarinas del Windmill Theatre de Londres ensayan con máscaras de gas y cascos metálicos. Excepto un cierre obligado de dos semanas en septiembre de 1939, el Windmill fue el único teatro londinense que permaneció abierto a lo largo de toda la guerra. Durante muchos años presumió de ello: "No hemos cerrado nunca".

Ballerine del Windmill Theatre, a Londra, provano con la maschera a gas e l'elmetto. A parte una chiusura obbligatoria di due settimane nel settembre del 1939, il Windmill fu l'unico teatro di Londra a rimanere aperto per tutta la guerra. Negli anni successivi proclamava orgoglioso: "Non abbiamo mai chiuso".

Kurt Hutton's portrait of the British singer, Vera Lynn. She was dubbed 'The Forces' Sweetheart'.

Fotografía de la cantante británica Vera Lynn tomada por Kurt Hutton. Se la llamaba "la novia del ejército".

La cantante inglese Vera Lynn in un ritratto di Kurt Hutton. Era stata soprannominata "la fidanzata dell'esercito".

The young Francis Albert Sinatra, gangly crooner from Hoboken, New Jersey, and darling of the bobbysoxers.

El joven Francis Albert Sinatra, el larguirucho cantante melódico de Hoboken (New Jersey), había robado el corazón a todas las adolescentes.

Il giovane Francis Albert Sinatra, lo smilzo cantante di Hoboken, New Jersey, che spezzava il cuore delle adolescenti.

2 June 1945. A delighted Josephine Baker embarrasses a British lance-corporal at a Victory party. Famous as a dancer and singer in the Thirties, Josephine Baker spent most of the war as a volunteer in the Free French Women's Air Auxiliary.

2 de junio de 1945. Una risueña Josephine Baker pone en una situación embarazosa a un caporal británico en una fiesta de celebración de la victoria. Conocida como cantante y bailarina en la década de 1930, Josephine Baker pasó la mayor parte de la guerra como voluntaria del cuerpo auxiliar del ejército femenino del aire en la Francia libre.

2 giugno 1945. Una divertita Josephine Baker mette in imbarazzo un caporale britannico durante una festa per la vittoria. Celebre cantante e ballerina negli anni Trenta, Josephine Baker fu, per la la maggior parte del periodo di guerra, una volontaria dell'aviazione della Francia libera.

May 1947. Lucille
Ball sings in the rain
at a New York
charity torchlight
procession.

Mayo de 1947.
Lucille Ball canta
bajo la lluvia en un
desfile con antorchas
para recoger fondos.

Maggio 1947.
Lucille Ball canta
sotto la pioggia
durante una
fiaccolata di
beneficienza a New
York.

Another dirty rat hits the canvas. Screen tough guy James Cagney practises his judo throws, July 1947.

Otro al suelo. James Cagney, el "duro" en la gran pantalla, hace una demostración de llaves de judo, en julio de 1947.

Un altro avversario al tappeto. James Cagney, il duro dello schermo, mostra la sua abilità di judoka nel luglio 1947.

'Here's another fine mess you've gotten me into…' Oliver Hardy in an unlikely role as a ballet star in the 1943 film *The Dancing Masters*.

"¡Ya me has metido en otro lío!" Oliver Hardy en un papel poco habitual como bailarina de ballet en la película *The Dancing Masters* en 1943.

"Mi hai messo ancora nei pasticci…" Oliver Hardy in un improbabile ruolo di stella della danza nel film *The Dancing Masters* del 1943.

Stan Laurel plays a
ballerina in the same
film, which was not
a great success, but
the routines had a
charm all their own.

Stan Laurel también
en el papel de
bailarina, en la
misma película, que
a pesar de no tener
mucho éxito valía
la pena por las
divertidas escenas
de ballet.

Nello stesso film,
Stan Laurel recita
nel ruolo di
ballerina. Il film non
fu un grande
successo ma le scene
di danza restano
memorabili.

Screen gangster becomes a football fan, November 1942. Like many Hollywood celebrities, Edward G Robinson (in profile, left) came to Europe to entertain Allied troops. The Studio bosses, most of them Jewish, encouraged their stars to do what they could in the struggle against Nazism.

El temido gángster de la gran pantalla se convierte en un aficionado más al fútbol, en noviembre de 1942. Al igual que muchas estrellas de Hollywood, Edward G. Robinson (izquierda, de perfil) vino a Europa para entretener a las tropas aliadas. Los dueños de los estudios cinematográficos, la mayoría de ellos judíos, animaron a sus estrellas a colaborar en la lucha contra el nazismo.

Il gangster del cinema diventa un appassionato di calcio, novembre 1942. Come molte celebrità di Hollywood anche Edward G. Robinson (a sinistra di profilo) raggiunse l'Europa per intrattenere i soldati alleati. I dirigenti degli Studios, in maggioranza ebrei, incoraggiavano le loro star a fare tutto il possibile nella lotta contro il nazismo.

October 1948. Ingrid Bergman and Alfred Hitchcock, off duty during the filming of *Under Capricorn*. They visited Bow Street, the Tower of London and the George at Southwark. The film was described as 'a pretty fair disaster'.

Octubre de 1948. Ingrid Bergman y Alfred Hitchcock, en un descanso del rodaje de la película *Atormentada*. Visitaron Bow Street, la Torre de Londres y el George de Southwark. El largometraje fue descrito como un "verdadero desastre".

Ottobre 1948. Ingrid Bergman e Alfred Hitchcock, durante una pausa del film *Il peccato di Lady Considine*. Visitarono Bow Street, la Torre di Londra e il George di Southwark. Il film fu un vero e proprio fiasco.

The biggest 'Hallo' in show business. Mickey Rooney arrives at Southampton on 1 January 1948 for an engagement at the London Palladium.

El saludo más grande del mundo del espectáculo. Mickey Rooney llega a Southampton el 1 de enero de 1948 para actuar en el London Palladium.

Il più grande "Hallo" dello spettacolo. Mickey Rooney al suo arrivo a Southampton, il 1° gennaio del 1948, per firmare un contratto al Palladium di Londra.

Sixteen-year-old Elizabeth Taylor joins the crowds to watch the Lord Mayor's Show, 1948. She had come to London to film *Conspirator*.

Elizabeth Taylor, con sólo 16 años de edad, se une a la multitud para asistir al Lord Mayor's Show, en 1948. Había venido a Londres con motivo del rodaje de *Traición*.

Elizabeth Taylor, all'epoca sedicenne, tra la folla che assiste al Lord Mayor's Show nel 1948. Era arrivata a Londra per girare il film *Alto tradimento*.

Yves Montand, French singer and actor, signs autographs for his fans in the summer of 1949. It was a good year for Montand. He met Simone Signoret, and fell in love with her at first sight, and was invited to sing at the wedding of Rita Hayworth and Ali Khan.

Yves Montand, actor y cantante francés, firma autógrafos a sus admiradoras en verano de 1949. Fue un buen año para Montand. Conoció a Simone Signoret y se enamoró de ella a primera vista, y fue invitado a cantar en la boda de Rita Hayworth y Ali Khan.

Yves Montand, cantante e attore francese, mentre firma degli autografi ai suoi ammiratori nell'estate del 1949. Il 1949 fu un buon anno per Montand: incontra Simone Signoret, della quale si innamora a prima vista, ed è invitato a cantare per la celebrazione del matrimonio tra Rita Hayworth e Ali Khan.

Between marriages: Rita Hayworth signs up for her fans, 1948. It was the year that she separated from her second husband Orson Welles, and the year in which she starred with him in *The Lady from Shanghai*. The following year she married Prince Ali Khan.

Entre dos bodas: Rita Hayworth firma autógrafos a sus admiradores, en 1948, el año en que se separó de su segundo marido, Orson Welles, y también el año en que trabajó con él en *La dama de Shanghai*. Al año siguiente se casó con Ali Khan.

Tra due matrimoni : Rita Hayworth distribuisce autografi a un gruppo di giovani ammiratori nel 1948. In quest'anno si separa dal secondo marito, Orson Welles, con il quale, nello stesso anno, ha recitato nel film *La signora di Shanghai*. L'anno successivo sposerà il principe Ali Khan.

8. Design for living
Diseño cotidiano
Arte di vivere

The man who re-drew the fashion books: French couturier Christian Dior poses with two of his models in 1949. Two years earlier he had introduced the 'New Look', featuring narrow shoulders and long, full skirts.

El hombre que rediseñó los libros de moda: el modisto francés Christian Dior posa con dos de sus modelos en 1949. Dos años antes había presentado el New Look, un estilo de líneas delgadas en los hombros y faldas largas y holgadas.

L'uomo che ridisegna i cataloghi della moda: lo stilista francese Christian Dior posa con due modelle nel 1949. Due anni prima aveva lanciato il New Look, che si caratterizzava per i vestiti con giacche attillate e gonne lunghe e ampie.

8. Design for living
Diseño cotidiano
Arte di vivere

The United States invasion of Europe had begun before the war. American design, culture and style had trickled across the Atlantic, bringing with it milk bars, streamlining, and cinemas built like Moorish palaces.

In the Forties the trickle became a flood. Hollywood led the way, for Hollywood was always at the forefront of fashion. The stars wore clothes and costumes that were as far removed from 'Austerity' and 'Utility' as chewing gum was from a carrot.

Until 1945, 'glamour' for Europeans meant 'uniform', but khaki serge has a limited appeal. For those that could afford it, one of the joys of peace was to return to out-and-out luxury. Christian Dior led the way with his 'New Look'. Architects once more put their dreams on paper, but capital was scarce in Europe and few dreams came true. In old-fashioned factories, swords were turned into ploughshares of pre-war design.

Science and technology leapt forward during the Forties. By the end of the decade, nations had at their disposal rocket propulsion, atomic power, the jet engine, radar, the earliest forms of artificial intelligence and the ballpoint pen. In some cases they didn't know what to do with their new toys. In others, sadly, they did.

La invasión estadounidense de Europa había empezado mucho antes de la guerra. El diseño, la cultura y el estilo norteamericanos habían cruzado el Atlántico llevando consigo *milk bars* (una especie de bares), diseños aerodinámicos y cines que parecían palacios.

En los años cuarenta se desató la gran invasión, con Hollywood como principal protagonista y forjador de nuevas modas. Las estrellas llevaban ropas tan alejadas de los ideales de austeridad y utilidad como un chicle lo puede estar de una zanahoria.

Hasta 1945, la palabra *glamour* significó "uniforme" para los europeos, pero la ropa caqui posee un atractivo limitado. Para los que podían permitírselo, la paz trajo consigo la posibilidad de volver al lujo sin restricciones. Christian Dior abrió nuevos caminos con su New Look. Una vez más, los arquitectos intentaron plasmar sus sueños sobre el papel, pero en Europa el capital era escaso y pocos de esos sueños se convirtieron en realidad. Así, en viejas fábricas, las espadas se convirtieron en arados con un diseño de antes de la guerra.

La ciencia y la tecnología avanzaron enormemente durante los años cuarenta. Hacia el final de la década, la humanidad disponía de cohetes, energía atómica, motores de reacción, radares, formas embrionarias de inteligencia artificial y bolígrafos. A veces no se sabía qué hacer con estos nuevos juguetes. Otras, desgraciadamente, sí se sabía qué utilidad darles.

L'invasione dell'Europa da parte degli Stati Uniti era cominciata prima della guerra. Il design, la cultura e lo stile americano avevano già attraversato l'Atlantico portando con sé i milk bar, nuove linee aerodinamiche e cinema che sembravano palazzi orientali.

Negli anni Quaranta quello che era stato un ruscello si trasforma in un fiume in piena. Hollywood, da sempre all'avanguardia nella moda, dà il segnale d'avvio. Le celebrità indossano vestiti e costumi che non hanno niente a che vedere con l'"austerità" e la "praticità".

Fino al 1945 per gli europei l'eleganza coincideva con l'"uniforme", ma i pantaloncini color cachi esercitavano ormai poco richiamo. Per chi se lo poteva permettere, una delle gioie del periodo di pace fu un ritorno a un lusso senza limiti. Christian Dior indicò la strada con il suo New Look. Ancora una volta gli architetti misero nero su bianco i propri sogni, ma i capitali scarseggiavano in Europa e pochi sogni si trasformarono in realtà. Nelle vecchie fabbriche le spade si trasformarono nelle lame degli aratri, come già nell'anteguerra.

La scienza e la tecnologia fecero enormi progressi durante gli anni Quaranta. Prima della fine del decennio l'umanità avrebbe conosciuto i razzi a propulsione, l'energia nucleare, i motori a reazione, i radar, le prime forme di intelligenza artificiale e le penne a sfera. In alcuni casi non si sapeva cosa fare di questi nuovi giocattoli, in altri – purtroppo – sì.

War time 'Utility', 1942. Clothes were rationed on a 'points' system which
assigned a value to articles and permitted customers to 'spend' a certain number
of total points, taking into account the type and amount of material used.

En 1942 primaba un diseño utilitario. Eran tiempos de guerra. La ropa también
sufrió racionamientos mediante un sistema de puntos que asignaba un valor a
los artículos y permitía a los clientes "gastar" una determinada cantidad de
puntos totales, según el tipo y la cantidad de material utilizado en cada prenda.

"Praticità" in tempo di guerra, 1942. I vestiti venivano razionati con un metodo
a "punti" che assegnava a ogni articolo un valore e permetteva agli acquirenti di
"spendere" un certo numero di punti. Il punteggio teneva conto del tipo e della
quantità dei materiali usati.

An elegant lady wearing Dior's 'New Look' gets a critical appraisal from a passer-by on the streets of London, 1949.

Una elegante dama vestida al estilo New Look de Christian Dior recibe la mirada crítica de una transeúnte en las calles de Londres, en 1949.

Una strada di Londra nel 1949. Una passante osserva con occhio clinico un'elegante signora che indossa una creazione New Look di Christian Dior.

Calculating both price and 'points'. A woman examines stockings after the introduction of clothes rationing. Clothes coupons (tickets entitling the holder to a ration), as well as food and petrol coupons, fed a busy and profitable black market.

Cómo calcular los precios y los "puntos" a la vez. Una mujer examina unas medias después de la introducción del racionamiento en los artículos de vestir. Los cupones para ropa (que autorizaban al titular a adquirir una "ración"), así como los cupones para comida y carburante, alimentaron un mercado negro dinámico y rentable.

Calcolare contemporaneamente prezzo e "punti". Una donna esamina delle calze dopo l'introduzione del razionamento dei vestiti. Le tessere annonarie (con biglietti che consentivano di ottenere una "razione"), riguardavano anche carburante e cibo e alimentarono un ricco e animato mercato nero.

July 1941. A solution to the problem of clothes rationing. Women in a Croydon store have their legs painted to resemble stockings. The 'points' thus saved could be used for other clothes.

Julio de 1941. Una solución al problema del racionamiento de ropa. Mujeres en una tienda de Croydon se dejan pintar las piernas para simular que llevan medias. Los "puntos" que así ahorraban podían utilizarlos para otras prendas.

Luglio 1941. Una soluzione per il problema del razionamento dei vestiti. Donne in un negozio Croydon si fanno dipingere le gambe simulando così di indossare le calze. I "punti" così risparmiati potevano essere usati per altri vestiti.

A British fashion show, March 1949. The show was primarily for overseas buyers. Desperate to boost exports, Britain was making a bold attempt to enter the international fashion market.

Un desfile de moda británico en marzo de 1949, organizado sobre todo para compradores norteamericanos. El Reino Unido, que deseaba aumentar sus exportaciones a toda costa, realizó un gran esfuerzo para entrar en el mercado internacional de la moda.

Una sfilata di moda britannica nel marzo 1949. Era destinata soprattutto ad acquirenti stranieri. Disperatamente bisognosa di sostenere le esportazioni, la Gran Bretagna fece di tutto per conquistare il mercato internazionale della moda.

November 1941.
Anne Scott James,
of the *Picture Post*
magazine, poses
for an article entitled
'Should Women
Wear Trousers?'
When this picture
was taken, hundreds
of thousands
already were.

Noviembre de 1941.
Anne Scott James,
de la revista *Picture
Post*, posa para un
artículo titulado
"¿Deben las mujeres
llevar pantalones?".
Cuando se tomó esta
foto, miles de ellas
ya los llevaban.

Novembre 1941.
Anne Scott James,
della rivista *Picture
Post*, posa per un
articolo intitolato
"Le donne possono
indossare i
pantaloni?" Quando
questa foto fu
scattata centinaia di
donne già lo
facevano.

July 1948. It was a glorious summer, and a wonderful time to be showing off new 'swimwear', although in those days you called them 'bathing costumes'. The bottle of wine, camera and binocular case indicate that this is one of Bill Brandt's posed fashion shots.

Julio de 1948. Fue un verano glorioso, y una magnífica oportunidad de lucir los bañadores, aunque en esa época se les llamaba "vestidos de baño". La botella de vino, la cámara fotográfica y los binoculares revelan que ésta es una de las fotografías preparadas de Bill Brandt.

Luglio 1948. Fu un'estate magnifica e particolarmente adatta a mostrare i nuovi costumi, che allora si chiamavano ancora "costumi da bagno". La bottiglia di vino, la macchina fotografica e l'astuccio per il binocolo, rivelano che si tratta di una studiata fotografia di moda di Bill Brandt.

July 1946.
A Casino de Paris
dancer models
the sensational
new 'bikini' at the
Molitor Pool in
Paris.

Julio de 1946. Una
bailarina del casino
de París presenta el
nuevo y sensacional
"biquini" en la
piscina de Molitor
de París.

Luglio 1946. Una
ballerina del Casino
de Paris presenta una
novità sensazionale,
il bikini, alla piscina
Molitor di Parigi.

Opera returns to
Glyndebourne.
Composer Benjamin
Britten (seated)
and singer Peter
Pears discuss a score.

La ópera vuelve
a Glyndebourne.
El compositor
Benjamin Britten
(sentado) y el
cantante Peter Pears
analizan una escena.

L'opera ritorna a
Glyndebourne.
Il compositore
Benjamin Britten
(seduto) e il cantante
Peter Pears
analizzano una
scena.

A nest of left-wing poets, 1949. From left to right: W H Auden, Cecil Day Lewis and Stephen Spender at a literary conference in Italy. Auden had spent the war years in the United States.

Tres escritores de izquierdas, en 1949. De izquierda a derecha: W.H. Auden, Cecil Day y Stephen Spender en un congreso de literatura en Italia. Auden pasó los años de guerra en EE.UU.

Tre scrittori di sinistra nel 1949. Da sinistra a destra: W. H. Auden, Cecil Day Lewis e Stephen Spender durante un congresso di letteratura in Italia. Auden aveva passato gli anni di guerra negli Stati Uniti.

January 1945. Children queue in Harrods for the autograph of
celebrated children's writer Enid Blyton. Her Noddy character was
still a few years away, but the Famous Five were well established.

Enero de 1945. Una multitud de niños hacen cola en los almacenes
Harrods para conseguir un autógrafo de la famosa escritora de libros
infantiles Enid Blyton. Su personaje Noddy tardaría aún algunos
años en aparecer, pero el Club de los Cinco era ya muy popular.

Gennaio 1945. Dei ragazzi fanno la coda da Harrods per avere
un autografo di Enid Blyton, celebre scrittrice per l'infanzia. Il
personaggio di Noddy sarebbe apparso alcuni anni dopo, ma la
Banda dei Cinque era già molto popolare.

Novelist and critic Pamela Hansford Johnson (left) talking with
novelist Olivia Manning (right) at the opening of the British PEN (Poets,
Essayists, Novelists) Club headquarters in Chelsea, February 1949.

La novelista y crítica literaria Pamela Hansford Johnson (izquierda)
charla con la novelista Olivia Manning (derecha) durante la
inauguración del británico PEN Club, un club de poetas, ensayistas
y novelistas, en Chelsea, en febrero de 1949.

La scrittrice e critica Pamela Hansford Johnson (a sinistra) s'intrattiene
con la collega Olivia Manning (a destra) all'inaugurazione del quartier
generale del PEN Club (Poets, Essayists, Novelists, cioè poeti, saggisti,
romanzieri), a Chelsea, nel febbraio del 1949.

Picasso in exile,
Paris 1948. The
artist had sworn not
to return to his
native Spain while
Franco ruled there.

Picasso en el exilio
en París, en 1948.
Este artista había
jurado no volver a
su España natal
mientras gobernara
Franco.

Picasso in esilio a
Parigi nel 1948.
L'artista aveva
giurato di non fare
ritorno in Spagna
finché Franco fosse
rimasto al governo.

Henry Moore, 1948. After working as an official war artist, Moore returned to his studies of semi-abstract female forms and family groups in the late 1940s.

Henry Moore, en 1948. Después de trabajar como artista de guerra oficial, Moore volvió a sus estudios de formas femeninas semiabstractas y de grupos familiares, a finales de la década de 1940.

Henry Moore, nel 1948. Dopo avere lavorato come artista ufficiale di guerra, Moore ritorna ai suoi studi semiastratti di donne e di gruppi familiari alla fine degli anni Quaranta.

Michael Redgrave chairs a meeting of Equity, the actors' trade union, in
1946. Some members are still in battledress. As with most other workers,
the war years had provided full employment for the acting profession.

Michael Redgrave preside una reunión del sindicato de actores Equity,
en 1946. Algunos asistentes todavía llevan uniformes. Al igual que en
otros sectores, la guerra había propiciado mucho empleo a estos
profesionales.

Michael Redgrave presiede un incontro dell'Equity, il sindacato degli
attori nel 1946. Alcuni partecipanti indossano ancora l'uniforme. Come
per altre professioni gli anni di guerra avevano garantito la piena
occupazione agli attori professionisti.

Abram Games with the poster he designed to attract recruits to the ATS. The women's army had previously been seen as less glamorous than the navy or air force.

Abram Games con el póster que diseñó para favorecer el alistamiento de mujeres en el ATS. Anteriormente, el ejército femenino había gozado de un prestigio inferior al de la marina o el ejército del aire.

Abram Games davanti a un manifesto disegnato per sollecitare il reclutamento nelle ATS. L'esercito femminile godeva allora di minor prestigio rispetto all'aviazione e alla marina.

A multiple exposure photograph of prima ballerina
Margot Fonteyn, 1949. As in the other arts, ballet
reached a far wider audience during the war, and its
appeal increased throughout the 1940s.

Una fotografía de exposición múltiple de la
excelente bailarina Margot Fonteyn, en 1949. Como
las otras artes, el ballet llegó a un público mucho
más amplio durante la guerra y su popularidad no
cesó de aumentar a lo largo de toda la década de
1940.

Montaggio fotografico della prima ballerina Margot
Fonteyn, nel 1949. Come tutte le arti anche il
balletto, durante la guerra, raggiunse un pubblico
più vasto e la sua popolarità non cessò di crescere
durante tutti gli anni Quaranta.

Forties triumphalism: the interior of an aeroplane hangar at Orbetello in Tuscany, designed by Italian architect and engineer Pier Luigi Nervi, 1940. Nervi used a latticework of reinforced concrete to create 'strength through form'.

El triunfalismo de los años cuarenta: el interior de un hangar de aviones en Orbetello, en la Toscana, obra del arquitecto e ingeniero italiano Pier Luigi Nervi, en 1940. Nervi utilizó un enrejado de hormigón armado para crear "fuerza a partir de la forma".

Trionfalismo anni Quaranta: l'hangar dell'aeroporto di Orbetello in Toscana, progettato dall'architetto e ingegnere Pier Luigi Nervi nel 1940. Nervi ha utilizzato un'ingraticciatura in cemento armato per creare "la forza attraverso la forma"

A soundproof room for acoustical research at the Bell Telephone Laboratories, Murray Hill, New Jersey. The walls, floor and ceiling are lined with fibreglass.

Una habitación insonorizada para investigaciones acústicas en los laboratorios de Bell Telephone, en Murray Hill (New Jersey). Las paredes, el suelo y el techo están forrados con fibra de vidrio.

Laboratorio insonorizzato per le ricerche acustiche dei Bell Telephone Laboratories, Murray Hill, New York, nel New Jersey. Le pareti, il pavimento e il tetto sono ricoperti con fibre di vetro.

Arctic Test. A 1948 Morris Oxford is put through
the freeze test. It had been left in 40 degrees of
frost for five days. The report proudly announced
that it started at 'the second time of asking'.

Una prueba polar. Un Morris Oxford de 1948
pasa la prueba de congelación. Ha estado a
40 grados bajo cero durante cinco días. El informe
afirmaba con orgullo que "arrancó a la segunda".

Esperimento polare. Una Morris Oxford del 1948
che è stata esposta per 5 giorni a -40 °C. Il
rapporto dichiara fieramente che si è accesa al
"secondo tentativo".

Lightning Test. Three million volts hit a car at the Westinghouse Electric Corporation, Pittsburgh. The passenger, happily, was unharmed.

Una prueba eléctrica. Una descarga de tres millones de voltios cae sobre un coche en la Westinghouse Electric Corporation, en Pittsburgh. El pasajero resultó ileso, afortunadamente.

Esperimento di conduttività. Una scarica di tre miloni di volt colpisce una macchina alla Westinghouse Electric Corporation a Pittsburgh. E, fortunatamente, il passeggero è rimasto indenne.

9. Sport and leisure
Deporte y entretenimiento
Sport e tempo libero

March 1943. Stanley Matthews takes a corner for the RAF. Matthews was labelled 'the best footballer the war has produced', but his greatest moment was to come in 1953, when he created three goals in 13 minutes in the FA Cup Final.

Marzo de 1943. Stanley Matthews lanza un saque de esquina para la RAF. Se le conocía como "el mejor futbolista que ha dado la guerra", pero su mejor momento no llegaría hasta 1953, cuando marcó tres goles en 13 minutos durante la final de la copa de la FA.

Marzo 1943. Stanley Matthews batte un corner per la RAF. Matthews fu definito il "miglior giocatore prodotto dalla guerra", ma il suo periodo d'oro sarebbe arrivato nel 1953 quando segnò tre gol in 13 minuti nella finale della coppa FA.

9. Sport and leisure
Deporte y entretenimiento
Sport e tempo libero

Even before the end of the war there were tasters of the sporting joys that lay ahead. Unofficial international matches were held, and crowds thronged to this less lethal rivalry. It hardly mattered what the sport was. Greyhound racing, speedway, TT (Tourist Trophy) motorcycle races, ice hockey, even the Oxford and Cambridge Boat Race attracted tens of thousands.

By 1946 sport had returned to normal. England's cricketers were thrashed by Australia, and their tennis players crashed out of the singles at Wimbledon. Liverpool were top of the Football League. The World Series had resumed in the States. Americans had won the four major golf tournaments. Joe Louis had emphasized his right to be World Heavyweight champion.

Grounds were packed. Fans had waited a long time to see their favourite teams in action again. Even the bottom clubs in the English Football League could guarantee gates of 15,000 week after week. Tragedy struck when over 65,000 people crammed into Burnden Park, Bolton, to see the game against Stoke. A barrier collapsed. Thirty-three people were killed.

The first post-war Olympic Games were held in London in 1948. The United States topped the table of medal winners, Sweden was second, France third. At the end of the Games a number of athletes from Eastern European countries defected to the West.

Incluso antes de que terminara la guerra se pudo disfrutar de las joyas deportivas que llegarían en el futuro. Se disputaban partidos internacionales no oficiales y las multitudes acudían en tropel a estos encuentros menos violentos. Poco importaba cuál fuera el deporte. Carreras de galgos, pruebas de velocidad, carreras de motocicletas del Tourist Trophy, hockey sobre hielo, incluso la regata entre Oxford y Cambridge atraía a las multitudes.

Hacia 1946 el deporte volvió a la normalidad. El equipo de críquet de Inglaterra fue derrotado por Australia y sus tenistas fueron eliminados de Wimbledon en la modalidad individual. Liverpool era líder de la liga inglesa de fútbol. Los World Series se habían retomado en EE.UU., los estadounidenses habían ganado los cuatro principales torneos de golf y Joe Louis había reclamado la legitimidad de su título de campeón del mundo de pesos pesados.

Los estadios estaban repletos. Los aficionados habían esperado mucho tiempo para volver ver a sus equipos favoritos en acción. Incluso los equipos más modestos de la liga de fútbol inglesa podían garantizar entradas de 15.000 personas semana tras semana. La tragedia estalló cuando más de 65.000 personas acudieron a Burnden Park, en Bolton, para ver el partido contra Stoke: una barrera se hundió y murieron 33 personas.

Los primeros Juegos Olímpicos después de la guerra se celebraron en Londres en 1948. EE.UU. acaparó el palmarés, Suecia quedó segunda y Francia tercera. Al final de los Juegos, numerosos atletas de Europa del Este huyeron a Occidente.

Anche prima della fine della guerra non si erano completamente perse le passioni legate allo sport. Si tenevano incontri internazionali amichevoli e le folle vi partecipavano appassionandosi a queste rivalità meno violente. Non importava molto quale disciplina fosse in gioco: corse di cani, gare motociclistiche del Tourist Trophy, hockey su ghiaccio, persino la classica regata tra Oxford e Cambridge attraeva decine di migliaia di persone.

Nel 1946 lo sport ritorna alla normalità. I giocatori di cricket della Gran Bretagna vengono sconfitti dall'Australia e i loro giocatori di tennis vengono eliminati nei singoli di Wimbledon. Il Liverpool è in testa alla classifica. Negli Stati Uniti ricominciano le World Series. Gli americani vincono le quattro maggiori competizioni di golf. Joe Louis ha definitivamente legittimato la vittoria al campionato mondiale dei pesi massimi.

Le gradinate si riempiono di nuovo. I tifosi avevano aspettato troppo tempo per vedere i loro idoli nuovamente in campo. Anche le squadre di bassa classifica del campionato inglese garantivano almeno 15.000 spettatori a incontro. Una tragedia si verificò al Bunden Park di Bolton dove si ammassarono 65.000 spettatori. Una barriera cedette improvvisamente e perirono 33 persone.

I primi giochi olimpici del dopoguerra si tennero a Londra nel 1948. Gli Stati Uniti furono i primi del medagliere, la Svezia seconda, la Francia terza. Alla fine dei giochi un certo numero di atleti, provenienti dai paesi dell'Europa orientale, passò all'Occidente.

November 1945. Ken Joy takes a 'bidon' of milk and
sugar during his successful bid to break the London to
Brighton cycle speed record.

Noviembre de 1945. Ken Joy toma un botellín con
leche y azúcar durante su afortunado intento de batir el
récord del trayecto entre Londres y Brighton en
bicicleta.

Novembre 1945. Ken Joy prende una bottiglietta di
latte e zucchero durante il tentativo, riuscito, di battere
il record di velocità sulla distanza Londra-Brighton.

December 1949. Von Bueren's cycle disintegrates as he wins the Swiss Championships in Zurich. Siegenthaler finishes second, but intact.

Diciembre de 1949. La bicicleta de Von Bueren se rompe en el momento de ganar el campeonato de Suiza celebrado en Zúrich. La de Siegenthaler no sufre desperfectos, pero éste queda en segunda posición.

Dicembre 1949. La bicicletta di von Bueren si disintegra al momento della vittoria del campionato svizzero a Zurigo. Siegenthaler arriva secondo, ma la sua bici resta sana.

A contentious issue in the 1990s: a *fait accompli* in the 1940s. The referee raises Miss Italy's hand in triumph after she knocks out Miss England in an unlikely-looking international tournament in Stockholm, 1949.

Un tema discutido en los noventa: un hecho consumado en los cuarenta. El árbitro levanta el brazo de Miss Italia en señal de victoria tras noquear a Miss Inglaterra en un singular torneo internacional celebrado en Estocolmo en 1949.

Un tema controverso negli anni Novanta: una consuetudine nei Quaranta. L'arbitro solleva, in segno di trionfo, la mano di Miss Italia che ha messo al tappeto Miss Inghilterra in un improbabile torneo internazionale a Stoccolma, 1949.

December 1947. World Heavyweight champion Joe Louis pins Jersey Joe Walcott against the ropes at Madison Square Garden, New York. Louis won on points. A year later he KO-ed Walcott. Two years later, Louis retired.

Diciembre de 1947. El campeón del mundo de los pesos pesados, Joe Louis, arrincona a Jersey Joe Walcott contra las cuerdas en el Madison Square Garden de New York. Louis ganó por puntos, un año después derrotó a Walcott por KO y dos años más tarde se retiró.

Dicembre 1947. Il campione del mondo dei pesi massimi Joe Louis stringe alle corde Jersey Joe Walcott al Madison Square Garden, New York. Louis vinse ai punti. L'anno successivo batté Walcott per KO. Due anni dopo Louis si ritirò.

Frank Swift, England's goalkeeper in the 1940s. He was among those killed in the Munich air crash of 1958.

Frank Swift, guardameta de la selección de Inglaterra en los años cuarenta. Swift estaba entre los que perecieron en el accidente de avión ocurrido en Múnich en 1958.

Frank Swift, portiere della nazionale inglese negli anni Quaranta. Fu tra le vittime dell'incidente aereo a Monaco nel 1958.

Emil Zátopek of
Czechoslovakia,
September 1947.
A year later he was
the surprise winner
of the 10,000 metres
at the London
Olympic Games.

El checoslovaco
Emil Zátopek, en
septiembre de 1947.
Un año después sería
el sorprendente
ganador de los
10.000 metros libres
en los Juegos
Olímpicos de
Londres.

Il ceco Emil
Zátopek, settembre
1947. Un anno
dopo, sorprendendo
tutti, vincerà la gara
dei 10.000 metri alle
Olimpiadi di
Londra.

American servicemen brought jitterbugging to Britain during the war. It became a craze. A couple step out at the Paramount Salon de Danse, Tottenham Court Road, London (above), while young beboppers hit the timber at the Club Eleven (right).

Durante la guerra, los militares estadounidenses llevaron al Reino Unido el *jitterbug,* que se convirtió en el baile de moda. En la foto superior, una pareja baila en el Paramount Salon de Danse, en Tottenham Court Road (Londres). En la foto de la derecha, una joven pareja baila *be-bop* en la pista del Club Eleven.

Durante la guerra i militari americani introdussero in Inghilterra il *jitterbug.* Diventò una mania. Una coppia balla al Paramount Salon de Danse, Tottenham Court Road, Londra (in alto), mentre giovani ballerini di be-bop battono i piedi sulla pista del Club Eleven (a destra).

Jitterbugging in
London, 1949.
To the old it was
depraved, to the
young it was joyous.

Dos londinenses
bailando *jitterbug* en
1949. Lo que para
los mayores era un
escándalo, para los
jóvenes era una gran
diversión.

Si balla il *jitterbug*
a Londra nel 1949.
Per gli anziani era
un ballo depravato,
per i giovani una
vera gioia.

Jitterbugging in
Paris, 1949.
The only difference
would appear to
be the footwear.

Dos parisinos
bailando *jitterbug*
en 1949. Parece que
la única diferencia
son los zapatos.

Anche a Parigi si
balla il *jitterbug*
nel 1949. L'unica
differenza è la scelta
delle scarpe.

Victory Leap. Young tennis players at an Essex junior championship,
August 1945. Sadly, ten years were to pass before an English
player was to win a Grand Slam championship. Angela Mortimer
won the French Open in 1955.

El salto de la victoria. Jóvenes tenistas durante un campeonato en
Essex, en agosto de 1945. Tuvieron que pasar diez años para que
un tenista británico ganara un campeonato del Grand Slam: Angela
Mortimer ganó el Open de Francia en 1955.

Il salto della vittoria. Giovani tennisti durante un campionato
giovanile nell'Essex, agosto 1945. Dovevano passare dieci anni
prima che un tennista inglese vincesse un campionato del grande
slam. Angela Mortimer vinse il French Open nel 1955.

The Playing Fields of Eton, November 1947. Collegers and Oppidans enjoy the mudbath of the Wall Game.

El área de juegos de Eton, en noviembre de 1947. Alumnos de un colegio público y sus compañeros de la escuela privada juegan al Wall Game de Eton, una especie de fútbol, y se divierten a lo grande revolcándose en el fango.

Il terreno di gioco di Eton nel novembre 1947. Collegiali di scuole pubbliche e private sguazzano nel fango durante una partita di pallamuro.

A holidaymaker
scans the horizon for
signs of the Cowes
Regatta, August
1949. The sweater
is the height of
Forties fashion.

Un veraneante
escruta el horizonte
en busca de alguna
embarcación de la
regata de Cowes, en
agosto de 1949. El
jersey que lleva era
la última moda en
los años cuarenta.

Gitanti scrutano
l'orizzonte durante
la regata di Cowes
nel 1949. Il gilet di
lana è il massimo
della moda negli
anni Quaranta.

The British seaside
two months after
D-day, August 1944.
Bournemouth begins
to return to normal.

Una playa británica
dos meses después
del día D, en
agosto de 1944.
Bournemouth
empieza a volver a
la normalidad.

Una spiaggia
britannica due mesi
dopo il D-day
nell'agosto 1944.
Bournemouth
ritorna lentamente
alla normalità.

The Games That Never Were. Japanese women display a banner decorated with pearls valued at £6,000. The Games were cancelled.

Los juegos que nunca se celebraron. Dos japonesas muestran un cartel decorado con perlas y valorado en 6.000 libras esterlinas. Los Juegos Olímpicos de 1940 fueron cancelados.

I giochi che non ebbero mai luogo. Una ragazza giapponese mostra una bandiera decorata con perle del valore di 6000 sterline. I giochi di Tokio furono annullati.

The last of a relay
of runners brings the
torch from Athens
into the stadium
at London for the
start of the 1948
Olympic Games.

El último de una
serie de corredores
que han traído la
antorcha olímpica
desde Atenas entra
en el estadio, en
Londres, para que
puedan dar
comienzo los Juegos
Olímpicos de 1948.

L'ultimo tedoforo
porta la torcia
olimpica, partita da
Atene, allo stadio di
Londra per
l'inaugurazione delle
Olimpiadi del 1948.

10. Children
Los más pequeños
Bambini

February 1940, east coast of England. The weapons of war were often treated as playground accessories by children, sometimes with disastrous results. For this boy, it would seem the worst that could happen would be to drop his ice cream.

Febrero de 1940, en la costa este de Inglaterra. Para los más pequeños, las armas de la guerra no eran a menudo más que fantásticos objetos para jugar, a veces con consecuencias desastrosas. Para el niño de la foto, lo peor que podría pasar es que se le cayera el helado.

Febbraio 1940, costa orientale dell'Inghilterra. Troppe volte le armi da guerra venivano considerate come giocattoli dai bambini, talvolta con risultati disastrosi. La maggiore preoccupazione del bambino nella foto sembra quella di non fare sgocciolare il gelato.

10. Children
Los más pequeños
Bambini

Babies like routine: children prefer a life that's spiced with the unexpected. And the early 1940s were full of the unexpected. For British boys and girls, there were disruptions at any time of the day or night: troops marching through town, air raids, bomb sites to explore, scrap metal to be collected for the 'war effort'. Schools were suddenly moved hundreds of miles to a safer location. Popular and unpopular teachers left to do their bit. Mums and dads were busy 20 hours out of the 24.

Pocket money was almost non-existent, but then, there was little enough to buy anyway. Toy factories were all turned over to war production, and after the war everything, it seemed, was 'for export' only. 'Make do and mend' applied every bit as much to playthings as to evening dresses or motor cars.

But what a time to fantasize! You could be Monty or Rommel in the desert, or an air ace in the Battle of Britain, or a film star like Betty Grable, or a heroine of the Resistance. You could march to glory, fight your way across whole continents, be a glamorous spy, save your comrades, even if it made you late for dinner.

But for many thousands of other children, reality was not fun, but death and disaster.

Mientras que los bebés aman la rutina, los niños prefieren lo extraordinario. Los primeros años de la década de 1940 fueron una sorpresa constante para los niños británicos, cuya vida cotidiana podía verse alterada en cualquier momento del día o la noche: soldados marchando a través de la ciudad, ataques aéreos, lugares bombardeados por explorar, trozos de metal para ser recogidos y coleccionados. Las escuelas se trasladaron de repente a cientos de kilómetros de donde estaban, a zonas más seguras. Los profesores tuvieron que partir hacia el frente. Los padres estaban ocupados 20 horas al día.

Casi no había dinero en circulación, aunque de todas formas tampoco había mucho que comprar. Las fábricas de juguetes producían armamento y tras la guerra parecía que todo estaba destinado exclusivamente "a la exportación". "Haz hacer y repara" era el lema que se aplicaba tanto a los juguetes como a los vestidos de noche o los automóviles.

Sin embargo, fue una buena época para dejar correr la imaginación. Uno podía ser Monty o Rommel en el desierto, un invencible piloto en la Batalla de Inglaterra, una estrella de cine como Betty Grable o incluso una heroína de la Resistencia. En las mentes de los más pequeños siempre había misiones urgentes que realizar, aunque se llegara tarde a la cena: desfilar hacia la gloria, abrirse paso a través de continentes enteros, ser un misterioso espía, salvar a los camaradas, etc.

Pero para muchos otros miles de niños la realidad no era tan divertida, sino que estaba llena de muerte y destrucción.

I bambini più piccoli sono abitudinari, i ragazzi più grandi invece amano una vita piena di sorprese. Gli inizi degli anni Quaranta sono pieni di sorprese. Per i ragazzi britannici ogni momento del giorno e della notte era pieno di novità: militari in marcia nelle città, bombardamenti aerei, crateri prodotti dalle bombe, schegge metalliche da raccogliere per lo "sforzo bellico". Le scuole improvvisamente furono spostate in luoghi più sicuri spesso a centinaia di chilometri dalla loro sede. I professori erano al fronte. Le mamme e i papà erano occupati 20 ore su 24.

I soldi della paghetta praticamente non esistevano e comunque non c'era quasi nulla da comprare. Le fabbriche di giocattoli si trasformarono in industrie militari e, dopo la guerra, ogni cosa sembrava prodotta esclusivamente "per l'esportazione". "Fallo aggiustare!" era la parola d'ordine tanto per i giocattoli quanto per i vestiti da sera o le automobili.

Ma quante occasioni per fantasticare! Potevi essere Monty o Rommel nel deserto, un asso dell'aviazione nella battaglia d'Inghilterra, una celebrità come Betty Grable oppure un'eroina della resistenza. Potevi marciare incontro alla gloria, o combattere attraverso interi continenti, essere una spia affascinante, salvare i tuoi commilitoni anche se qualche volta arrivavi un po' tardi per la cena.

Ma per migliaia di altri bambini e ragazzi la realtà non fu affatto divertente e significò soltanto orrore e morte.

1940. Evacuee children take a last look at families and London before leaving for the countryside. One and a half million children were evacuated. Some enjoyed their new world, but many felt the strain of living with strangers in a land at war.

1940. Unos niños dicen adiós a sus familiares de Londres antes de partir hacia el campo, un lugar más seguro. Se evacuaron más de un millón y medio de niños y niñas. A algunos les gustó su nueva forma de vida, pero muchos no llegaron a acostumbrarse a vivir con extraños en un país en guerra.

1940. Alcuni bambini danno l'ultimo saluto alle famiglie a Londra prima di partire per la campagna. Furono trasferiti un milione e mezzo di ragazzi. Alcuni apprezzarono il nuovo stile di vita, ma la maggioranza non si abituò mai a vivere con degli estranei in un paese in guerra.

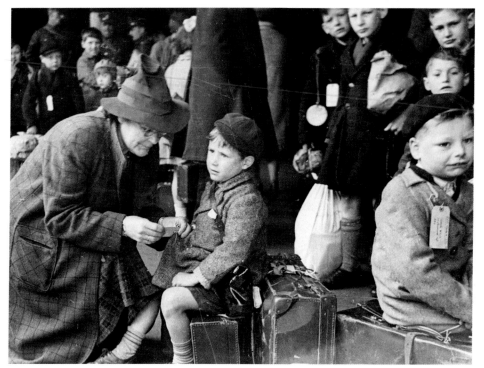

A happier journey: a volunteer helper fastens an identification label onto a child's coat at Paddington Station, May 1942. The children in this picture by Bert Hardy were going on holiday, not being evacuated.

Un viaje más feliz: una voluntaria coloca una etiqueta identificativa en el abrigo de un niño en la estación de Paddington, en mayo de 1942. Los niños de esta foto, tomada por Bert Hardy, no eran evacuados, sino que iban de vacaciones.

Un viaggio più felice: un'ausiliaria attacca un'etichetta d'identificazione sul cappotto di un bambino alla Paddington Station, maggio 1942. I ragazzi ritratti in questa foto di Bert Hardy non sono sfollati, stanno andando in vacanza.

July 1940. A ten-year-old girl, recently evacuated from the Channel port of Folkestone, helps out on a farm at Llanvetherine, near Abergavenny, Wales. There were many stories of the disbelief with which town children greeted the wonders of nature.

Julio de 1940. Una niña de diez años, recientemente evacuada del puerto de Folkestone, en el canal de la Mancha, ordeña una vaca en una granja de Llanvetherine, cerca de Abergavenny, en Gales. Innumerables historias relatan la emoción que sintieron los niños de la ciudad al entrar en contacto con la naturaleza.

Luglio 1940. Una ragazza di dieci anni, da poco sfollata dal porto di Folkestone, sulla Manica, lavora in una fattoria a Llanvetherine, vicino Abergavenny nel Galles. Si diffusero moltissime storielle sull'incredulità dei bambini di città davanti alle meraviglie della natura.

Refreshment for
the thirsty. A young
evacuee takes a
glass of milk during
her journey.

Un remedio contra
la sed. Una niña
evacuada toma un
vaso de leche
durante el viaje.

Un rimedio contro
la sete. Una bambina
sfollata beve un
bicchiere di latte
durante il viaggio.

Schoolchildren form orderly files to march away from their concrete
shelters after a practice alarm at Southgate, London, at the height of
the Blitz. Shelters came in many shapes, sizes and materials.

Los escolares forman en orden al salir de sus refugios de hormigón
en un simulacro de alarma en Southgate (Londres), en el punto
álgido del *Blitz,* los ataques aéreos sobre la capital británica. Había
refugios de formas, tamaños y materiales muy diversos.

Un gruppo di scolari forma una fila ordinata nel lasciare un rifugio
di cemento dopo un'esercitazione a Southgate, Londra, nel periodo
più aspro dei bombardamenti tedeschi. I rifugi erano costruiti in
tutte le forme e dimensioni e utilizzando i materiali più diversi.

The original caption to this photograph reads: 'A family gives the thumbs up to a warden who warned them of a delayed action bomb he found in the vicinity of south east London.' In reality, the primitive shelter would have been of little help.

El pie de foto original de esta foto es: "Una familia levanta los pulgares a un guardia que les había avisado de que se había encontrado una bomba sin explotar en los alrededores, en el sureste de Londres". Si hubiera explotado, su precario refugio no habría servido de nada.

La didascalia originale di questa foto diceva: "Una famiglia alza i pollici a una guardia che li aveva messi in guardia su una bomba trovata intatta nelle vicinanze, nel sud-est di Londra." In caso di esplosione questo rifugio casalingo sarebbe stato di scarso aiuto.

Newly created playground, 1946. Children play on a bomb site in
the East End of London, just after the war. For many years the
rubble and disorder of such areas fed the imagination of children.

Otro sitio para jugar, 1946. Unos niños juegan en las ruinas de
una casa bombardeada en el East End de Londres, poco después
de la guerra. Durante muchos años, los escombros y el desorden
de lugares como éste alimentaron la imaginación de los niños.

Un nuovo luogo per giocare, 1946. Bambini che giocano in una
zona bombardata dell'East End di Londra, poco dopo la fine della
guerra. Per anni le macerie e il disordine di aree simili avrebbero
continuato ad alimentare l'immaginazione dei ragazzi.

Newly destroyed
home, 1941.
An orphan in
Belarus, former
Soviet Union, cries
outside his shattered
family home.

Otro hogar
destruido, en 1941.
En la población de
Bielorrusia, en la
antigua Unión
Soviética, un
huérfano llora ante
su casa en ruinas.

Una casa appena
distrutta nel 1941.
In Bielorussia,
nell'ex Unione
Sovietica, un orfano
piange davanti ai
resti della sua casa.

Young members of a
Nazi Youth group
proudly display their
flags at an open-air
camp near Berlin,
1940.

Jóvenes miembros
de un grupo de las
juventudes nazis
enarbolan orgullosos
sus banderas en un
campo al aire libre
cerca de Berlín, en
1940.

Giovani membri
di un'unità della
Gioventù nazista
impugnano
orgogliosamente
le bandiere in un
campo all'aperto
vicino a Berlino,
1940.

Children gather
behind a barbed
wire fence at
Auschwitz in the last
few days of the war.

Un grupo de niños
reunidos ante una
alambrada en
Auschwitz durante
los últimos días de
la guerra.

Alcuni ragazzi si
raccolgono dietro
un recinto in filo
spinato ad Auschwitz
pochi giorni prima
della fine della
guerra.

A Yugoslavian child
gives a hesitant Nazi
salute to a German
soldier, 1941.
The Yugoslav Royal
Army surrendered
on 17 April.

Un niño yugoslavo
realiza un tímido
saludo nazi a un
soldado alemán, en
1941. El ejército real
yugoslavo se rindió
el 17 de abril de ese
año.

Un bambino
yugoslavo fa un
esitante saluto
nazista a un soldato
tedesco, 1941.
L'esercito reale
yugoslavo si era
arreso il 17 aprile.

Thanksgiving Day, London, 26 November 1942. A US sergeant distributes candy to an ever-growing crowd of East End children. It wasn't long before every American serviceman was greeted with the phrase 'Got any gum, chum'.

El día de acción de gracias, en Londres, el 26 de noviembre de 1942. Un sargento estadounidense reparte caramelos entre una creciente multitud de niños en East End. No faltaba mucho para que la frase de bienvenida a todos los soldados del GI fuera "¿Tiene un chicle, señor?".

Il giorno del ringraziamento a Londra, 26 novembre 1942. Un sergente americano distribuisce dolciumi a una folla crescente di bambini dell'East End. Di lì a poco tutti i soldati americani sarebbero stati accolti dal ritornello "Signore, dammi un chewing gum".

The thrills of the Saturday morning matinée. Children queue
for tickets at the Gaumont State Cinema, Kilburn, 1946.

La emoción de la sesión matinal del sábado. Un grupo de
niños hacen cola para sacar entradas en el cine Gaumont
State, en Kilburn, en 1946.

Il brivido del cinema la domenica mattina. Alcuni ragazzi
fanno la coda per comprare il biglietto al Gaumont State
Cinema, Kilburn, 1946.

An infra-red
photograph of
a Saturday matinée.
Even in the 1940s
there was concern
about the diet
of fantasy and gun-
toting drama.

Una fotografía de
infrarrojos en una
sesión matinal del
sábado. Incluso en
los años cuarenta se
procuraba no
mostrar escenas de
violencia a los
pequeños.

Una foto ai raggi
infrarossi durante
una proiezione della
domenica mattina.
Anche durante gli
anni Quaranta si
cercava di evitare le
scene violente nei
film per bambini.

The spoils of war, September 1940. Children in a south London street sort through fragments of shrapnel. Offically, such finds would be collected as part of the national war effort, but many found their way into private collections.

Jugando con el botín de guerra, en septiembre de 1940. En una calle del sur de Londres, un grupo de niños recoge fragmentos de obús. En principio debían ser recogidos por las autoridades, pero muchos pasaron a formar parte de colecciones privadas.

Bottino di guerra, settembre 1940. In una strada nel sud di Londra alcuni bambini raccolgono schegge di una granata. Ufficialmente le schegge venivano raccolte per lo sforzo bellico nazionale, ma molte venivano conservate per le proprie collezioni private.

Lunchtime at a
Düsseldorf school,
1946. The city was
to become the
richest in Germany,
but that lay
generations ahead.

La hora del
almuerzo en una
escuela de
Düsseldorf en 1946.
Esta ciudad se
convertiría en la más
rica de Alemania,
pero aún faltaban
varias generaciones
para ello.

Pranzo in una scuola
di Düsseldorf nel
1946. La città
diventerà la più ricca
della Germania, ma
soltanto qualche
generazione dopo.

Hungarian boys outside their school, April 1945. The war in Europe is about to end. Hope has yet to come.

Niños húngaros en el exterior de su escuela, en abril de 1945. La guerra en Europa toca a su fin, pero la esperanza todavía no ha renacido.

Ragazzi ungheresi all'uscita della scuola, aprile 1945. La guerra in Europa sta per finire. La speranza deve ancora arrivare.

January 1940. London children line up for a regulation spoonful of medicine from their teacher, Mr Jones. The children had been evacuated with their teacher and his wife to Heyshott in Sussex.

Enero de 1940. Un grupo de niños y niñas hacen cola para que el profesor, Mr. Jones, les administre una cucharada de medicina. Junto con el profesor y su esposa, habían sido evacuados a Heyshott, en Sussex.

Gennaio 1940. Piccoli londinesi fanno la coda perché il maestro, Mr. Jones, possa somministrare loro un cucchiaio di medicina. Gli scolari erano sfollati con il maestro e sua moglie a Heyshott nel Sussex.

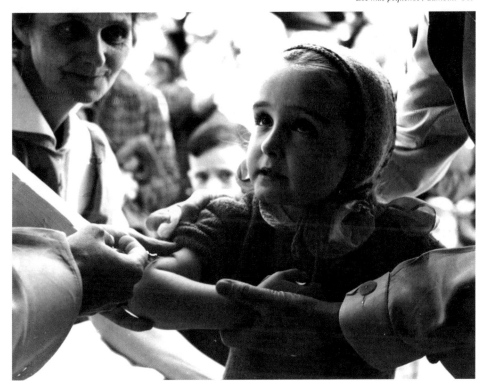

December 1943. An apprehensive young girl receives her immunization injection against diphtheria. Plans were already being made for the brave new world that would be created once the war was over.

Diciembre de 1943. Una niña asustada es vacunada contra la difteria. En esta época ya se estaban haciendo planes para el nuevo mundo que iba a crearse una vez terminada la guerra.

Dicembre 1943. Una preoccupata bambina riceve un'iniezione di vaccino contro la difterite. Si stanno già mettendo le basi per quel nuovo mondo che si sarebbe creato alla fine della guerra.

11. All human life
Cosas de la vida
Fatti della vita

'There was an old man with a beard, who said, It is just as I feared! Two owls and a hen, four larks and a wren have all built their nests in my beard.' A disciple of Edward Lear faces the rigours of 1940.

"Había una vez un anciano con barba que dijo: 'Es tal como había temido que sucediera. Dos búhos, una gallina, cuatro alondras y un carrizo han construido su nido en mi barba'." Un discípulo de Edward Lear hace frente a los rigores de 1940.

"C'era un vecchio con la barba che diceva: 'È proprio come temevo! Due civette e una gallina, quattro allodole e un'anatrina hanno fatto il nido nella mia barba!'." Un discepolo di Edward Lear affronta i rigori del 1940.

11. All human life
Cosas de la vida
Fatti della vita

You didn't have to go far to find weirdness during the 1940s. Much of it was born of the war. People found themselves in situations that were unusual, unbearable, unfathomable. Such situations brought out the eccentric in the species.

It was a great age for trying to turn aside horror with humour. People wore funny clothes and gadgets. They put silly labels on their homes, their vegetables, their animals. They adapted the debris of war to novel and bizarre uses.

A lot of it was unintentional. If there was an air raid and a gas alert, you had to put on your tin helmet and your gas mask. With no petrol available, you felt compelled to turn your bicycle into a coal lorry, a delivery van, a taxi. Much of the humour, however, was deliberate. And there was often a photographer casting about for a picture that would bring a smile to the face of editor and reader.

If all else failed, you could find a man who could bend iron bars with his teeth, or lift incredible weights, or had a novel use for his hat, his beard, his trouser turn-ups. Women seemed not to bother with this sort of thing.

En los años cuarenta no era necesario ir muy lejos para ver rarezas. Muchas de ellas nacieron de la guerra misma. A menudo la gente se encontraba en situaciones insólitas, insoportables e insondables que hacían emerger lo más excéntrico de la especie humana.

Fue una buena época para intentar vencer el horror con el humor. Las gentes llevaban ropa divertida y objetos singulares. Ponían nombres ridículos a sus casas, plantas y animales y daban a los deshechos producidos por la guerra usos nuevos y extravagantes.

Buena parte de estos comportamientos eran involuntarios. Si se producía un ataque aéreo o una alarma de gas, uno debía ponerse un casco metálico y una máscara de gas. Sin carburante, la bicicleta se convertía en un camión para transportar carbón, en una furgoneta de reparto o incluso en un taxi. Sin embargo, la mayoría de las situaciones cómicas eran deliberadas y a menudo había cerca un fotógrafo listo para inmortalizar una escena que hiciera sonreír a los editores y a los lectores.

Si todo lo demás fallaba, siempre podía encontrarse un hombre capaz de doblar barras de hierro con los dientes, levantar enormes pesos o descubrir nuevos usos para su sombrero, su barba o la vuelta de los pantalones. Es curioso que las mujeres no se entretuvieran tanto con este tipo de cosas.

Non c'è bisogno di cercare lontano per trovare situazioni stravaganti durante gli anni Quaranta. Molte di queste furono determinate dalla guerra. La gente si trovò in circostanze insolite, intollerabili, insondabili. Circostanze che portarono la specie umana a comportamenti eccentrici.

Fu un'epoca ideale per tentare di rimuovere l'orrore apprezzando il lato comico delle cose. La gente indossava abiti e accessori ridicoli. Metteva alle loro case, alle verdure, agli animali le etichette più improbabili. Trasformava i disagi della guerra in usi nuovi e bizzarri.

La maggior parte delle stranezze si realizzava inconsciamente. Se c'era un raid aereo o un allarme per l'attacco coi gas si doveva necessariamente indossare l'elmetto e la maschera antigas. In mancanza di carburante si era costretti a trasformare la propria bicicletta in un carro per il carbone, in una camionetta per le consegne, in un taxi. Gli aspetti più comici, comunque, si operavano consapevolmente. E spesso c'erano fotografi alla ricerca di immortalare una scena che avrebbe strappato un sorriso all'editore e al lettore.

Quando niente sembra funzionare, non è difficile trovare qualcuno capace di piegare una sbarra di ferro con i denti o sollevare pesi incredibili o sperimentare una nuova funzione per il proprio cappello, la barba, le bretelle. Le donne invece sembravano meno coinvolte in questo tipo di cose.

Blindfold training for fire crews in Germany. The German firemen
are being trained to follow the sound of a gong. Three seem certain to
pass the test; one looks set to fail.

Entrenamiento a ciegas en Alemania. Cuatro bomberos alemanes se
entrenan al son de un gong. Tres parece que pasarán la prueba; uno de
ellos anda un poco despistado.

Pompieri mascherati fanno un'esercitazione in Germania. Gli uomini si
stanno esercitando a indovinare la provenienza del suono di un gong.
Tre di loro sembra che passeranno la prova, l'altro non sembra avere
scampo.

Blindfold training for fire crews in Britain. The British firemen are practising feeling their way in total darkness while wearing respirators.

Entrenamiento a ciegas en Reino Unido. Los bomberos británicos aprenden a encontrar el camino en plena oscuridad y llevando aparatos de respiración.

Pompieri mascherati fanno un'esercitazione in Gran Bretagna. Gli uomini si esercitano a orientarsi nella totale oscurità mentre indossano maschere per la respirazione artificiale.

Gallant British War Effort, One: Sixty-year-old Home Guard Sergeant Gander balances a 130lb (60 kilo) bar on his head.

Valiente esfuerzo de guerra británico, primera parte: el sargento Gander de la fuerza de reserva, de 60 años, mantiene en equilibrio sobre la cabeza una barra de 60 kilos.

Gagliardo sforzo di guerra britannico, il sergente Gander, militare di riserva di 60 anni, solleva con la testa un bilanciere di 60 chilogrammi.

Gallant British War Effort, Two: Home Guardsman Joe Price, a blacksmith by trade, bends an iron bar with his teeth.

Valiente esfuerzo de guerra británico, segunda parte: Joe Price, de la fuerza de reserva y herrero de profesión, dobla una barra de hiero con los dientes.

Gagliardo sforzo di guerra britannico, due: Joe Price, militare di riserva, fabbro nella vita civile, piega una sbarra di ferro con i denti.

Life in a gas mask.
A Gloucester
policeman on traffic
duty, March 1941.

Cómo vivir con una
máscara de gas: un
policía de Gloucester
regulando el tráfico,
en marzo de 1941.

Vivere con la
maschera a gas.
Un poliziotto di
Gloucester dirige
il traffico, marzo
1941.

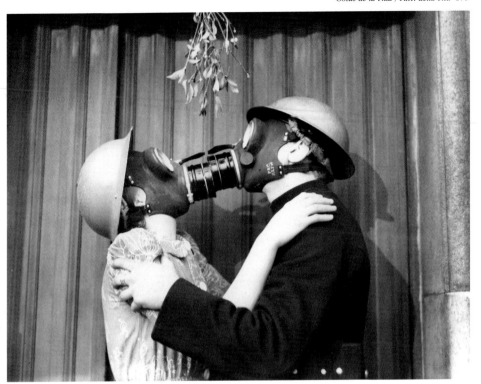

A member of the Auxiliary Fire Service takes a break from the Blitz, Christmas 1940. To many, there was something comic about the gas mask, and the many things you couldn't do while wearing one.

Un miembro del cuerpo auxiliar de bomberos descansa un momento durante el *Blitz*, los ataques aéreos sobre Londres, en las Navidades de 1940. Para muchos había algo cómico en las máscaras de gas y, sobre todo, en todo lo que no podía hacerse llevándolas.

Un membro del Servizio ausiliario antincendio durante una pausa dei bombardamenti, Natale 1940. Per molti c'era un che di comico nell'uso della maschera e nelle cose che, indossandola, rendeva difficile fare.

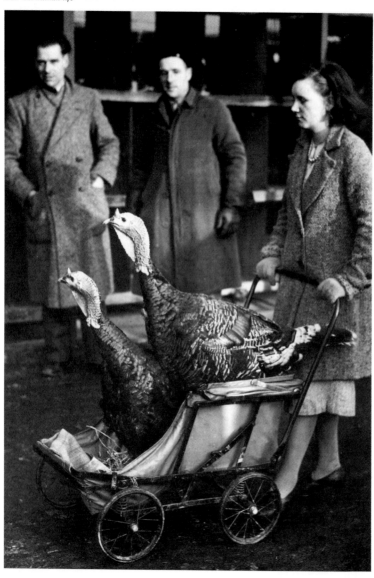

December 1940.
A woman takes her
Christmas turkeys
home from
Maidstone market.
People were less
squeamish about
doing their own
slaughtering in the
1940s.

Diciembre de 1940.
Una mujer
transporta unos
pavos para la cena
de Navidad
comprados en
el mercado de
Maidstone. En los
años cuarenta la
gente tenía menos
escrúpulos a la
hora de sacrificar
animales para comer.

Dicembre 1940. Una
donna trasporta i
tacchini per la cena
di Natale dal
mercato di
Maidstone. Negli
anni Quaranta le
persone diventarono
meno scrupolose
nell'ammazzare da
sé gli animali.

Not as innocent as it appears. These salmon had been poached from a local stream in September 1943.

No es tan inocente como parece. Estos salmones han sido pescados ilegalmente en un río cercano, en septiembre de 1943.

Meno innocente di quanto sembri: i salmoni della foto sono stati pescati illegalmente in un fiume nei dintorni nel settembre del 1943.

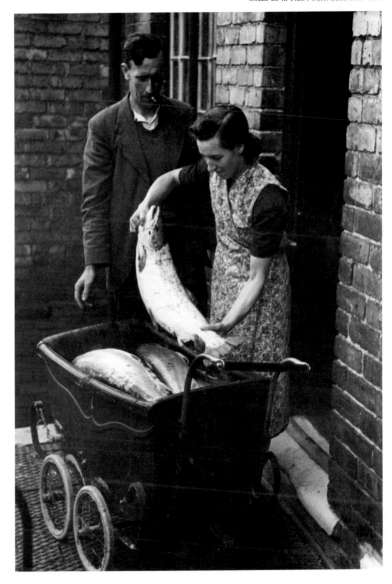

Georgie Porky. His Majesty King George VI
and one of his prize pigs regard each other
on the royal farm at Windsor, August 1942.
The King survived the war: the pig didn't.

Jorgito el cerdito. Su majestad el rey Jorge VI
y uno de sus cerdos se miran frente a frente
en la granja real de Windsor, en agosto de
1942. El rey sobrevivió a la guerra; el cerdo
tuvo otra suerte.

Georgie il porco. Sua maestà il re Giorgio VI,
e uno dei suoi premiati maiali si guardano
negli occhi nella fattoria reale di Windsor,
agosto 1942. Il re sopravvisse alla guerra, il
maiale no.

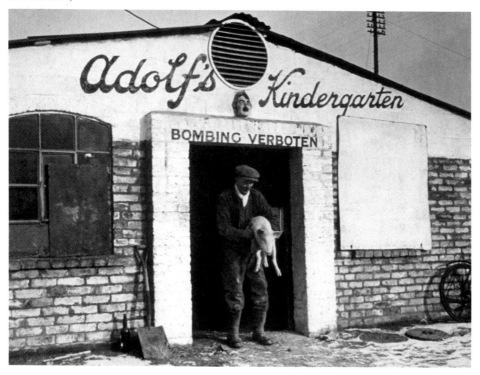

A dustman from Tottenham, London, holds one of his pigs (above). Pig-raising was s.rongly encouraged during the war. The little pig (right) was allegedly christened Hitler by its owner after it had tried to grab all the food from the rest of the litter.

Un basurero de Tottenham, en Londres, sostiene uno de sus cerdos (superior). Las autoridades incentivaron la cría de cerdos durante la guerra. En la foto de la derecha, un cerdo bautizado con el nombre de Hitler por su dueño después de que intentara coger toda la comida de entre los desperdicios.

Uno spazzino di Tottenham, a Londra, tiene in braccio uno dei suoi maiali (in alto). L'allevamento dei maiali fu fortemente incoraggiato durante la guerra. Il maialino (a destra) fu battezzato dal proprietario Hitler perché aveva tentato di arraffare il cibo dai resti della spazzatura.

Fantasy football.
A pet parrot helps
its owner fill in a
wartime football
pool coupon.

Una original manera
de tentar a la suerte.
Un loro ayuda a su
dueño a rellenar una
quiniela durante la
guerra.

Fantasie da
totocalcio. Un
pappagallo aiuta
il suo proprietario
a compilare una
schedina durante
la guerra.

Waiting for the
'All Clear'. A bush
baby shelters in a tea
mug, March 1941.

Esperando a que
cese el peligro. Un
gálago busca refugio
en una taza de té, en
marzo de 1941.

Aspettando che il
pericolo passi. Un
galagone si rifugia
in una tazza di tè,
marzo del 1941.

The Long and the Short of it: the world's tallest man, Ian van Albert, nine feet (3 metres) tall, poses beside George Aslett, who measures three feet (1 metre).

El gigante y el enano. El hombre más alto del mundo, Ian van Albert, de tres metros, posa junto a George Aslett, que mide apenas uno.

Il nano e il gigante: l'uomo più alto del mondo (3 metri), Ian van Albert, fotografato accanto a George Aslett, alto appena un metro.

January 1940.
A team of midgets
from the Earl's
Court Circus give
a helping hand to
the goalkeeper
at Fulham football
ground.

Enero de 1940. Un
grupo de enanos del
circo de Earl's Court
ayudan a detener un
balón al portero, en
el terreno de juego
de Fulham.

Gennaio 1940.
Una squadra di
piccoli tifosi
dell'Earl's Court
Circus dà una mano
al portiere nello
stadio di Fulham.

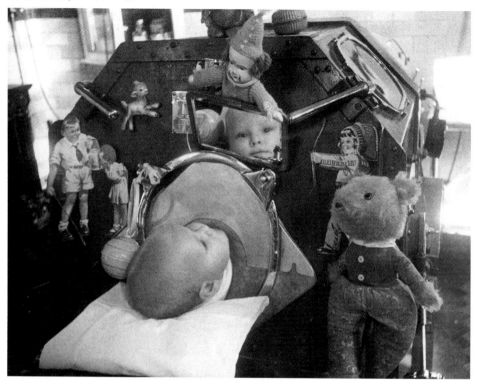

Life in an 'iron lung'. A 16-month-old child at the Western Fever Hospital, London, July 1947 (above). The child's condition was improving and he was able to breathe normally for six hours a day. Kenneth Evans (right), a paralysed engineer, uses a microfilm device to enable him to read books.

La vida en un pulmón de acero. Un bebé de 16 meses en el hospital Western Fever de Londres, en julio de 1947 (superior). Su enfermedad mejoraba y ya podía respirar normalmente durante seis horas al día. En la foto de la derecha, Kenneth Evans, un ingeniero paralizado, utiliza un sistema de microfilmes para leer libros.

Vivere in un polmone d'acciaio. Un bambino di 16 mesi al Western Fever Hospital di Londra, luglio 1947 (in alto). Le sue condizioni di salute stanno migliorando ed è già capace di respirare autonomamente per sei ore al giorno. Kenneth Evans (a destra), un ingegnere paralizzato, utilizza un sistema di microfilm che gli permette di leggere.

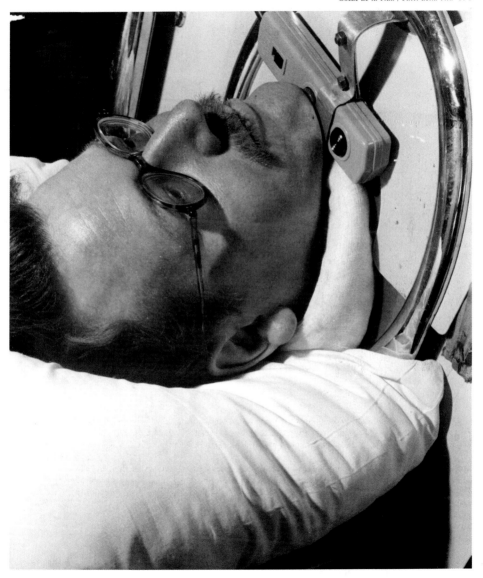

Hi-tech. The great-grandfather of all computers, January 1948. The control
desk of the IBM Selective Sequence Electronic Calculator, New York. It was then
the world's fastest calculator, one thousand times faster than any other.

Alta tecnología. El tatarabuelo de los ordenadores en enero de 1948. Una
operadora sentada en la mesa de control del calculador electrónico de secuencia
selectiva de IBM, en Nueva York. Por aquel entonces era el ordenador más
rápido del mundo, mil veces más rápido que cualquier otro.

Alta tecnologia. Il capostipite di tutti i computer, gennaio 1948. La consolle di
controllo di un calcolatore elettronico di sequenza selettiva dell'IBM, New York.
Era all'epoca il calcolatore più veloce del mondo, mille volte più rapido di tutti
gli altri modelli.

Eye-tech. A soldier undergoes an eye examination, 1945.

Alta tecnología desde otro punto de vista. Un soldado pasa una revisión ocular, en 1945.

Un'altra forma di alta tecnologia: un soldato si sottopone all'esame della vista, 1945.

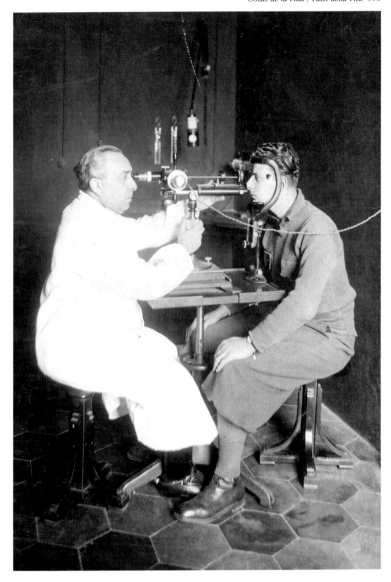

Index

How to buy or license a picture from this book

The pictures in this book are drawn from the extensive archives of The Hulton Getty Picture Collection, originally formed in 1947 as the Hulton Press Library. The Collection contains approximately 15 million images, some of which date from the earliest days of photography. It includes original material from leading press agencies – Topical Press, Keystone, Central Press, Fox Photos and General Photographic Agency as well as from *Picture Post*, the *Daily Express* and the *Evening Standard*.

Cómo adquirir copias u obtener autorización para reproducir las imágenes.

Las fotografías incluidas en esta obra forman parte del extenso archivo de "The Hulton Getty Picture Collection", reunido en 1947 con el nombre original de "the Hulton Press Library". Esta colección está integrada por unos quince millones de imágenes aproximadamente, algunas de las cuales se remontan a los primeros días de la fotografía. El archivo se compone de material original procedente de las principales agencias de prensa estadounidenses y británicas, tales como Topical Press, Keystone, Central Press, Fox Photos y General Photographic Agency, así como de otras fotografías aparecidas en publicaciones británicas como el *Picture Post*, el *Daily Express* y el *Evening Standard*.

Come comprare o noleggiare le foto di questo libro

Le foto di questo libro fanno parte del grande archivio "The Hulton Getty Picture Collection", raccolto a partire dal 1947 originariamente come "the Hulton Press Library". La collezione comprende circa quindici milioni di immagini alcune delle quali risalgono ai primissimi tempi della fotografia. L'archivio si compone di materiale originale proveniente dalle maggiori agenzie giornalistiche americane e britanniche come Topical Press, Keystone, Central Press, Fox Photos e General Photographic Agency e di altre immagini apparse sulle pubblicazioni britanniche *Picture Post*, *Daily Express* ed *Evening Standard*.

Picture Licensing Information

To license the pictures listed below please call Getty Images + 44 171 266 2662 or email info@getty-images.com your picture selection with the page/reference numbers.

Hulton Getty Online

All of the pictures listed below and countless others are available via Hulton Getty Online at:
http://www.hultongetty.com

Buying a print

For details of how to purchase exhibition-quality prints call The Hulton Getty Picture Gallery + 44 171 376 4525 (fax) +44 171 376 4524 hulton.gallery@getty-images.com

Información sobre licencias

Puede solicitar la licencia de las fotos que se relacionan a continuación a través del teléfono 00 44 171 266 2662, o un mensaje de correo electrónico a la dirección info@getty-images.com. Indique los números de referencia y de página de las imágenes que desea.

Hulton Getty Online

Puede encontrar estas imágenes y otras muchas en la *web* de la Hulton Getty Online:
http://www.hultongetty.com

Adquisición de copias

Para obtener más infomación acerca de cómo adquirir reproducciones para exposiciones, póngase en contacto con The Hulton Getty Picture Gallery, a través del teléfono 00 44 171 376 4525. (fax) +44 171 376 4524 hulton.gallery@getty-images.com

Informazioni per il noleggio

Per noleggiare le immagini elencate in basso telefonare allo 00 44 171 266 2662, o inviare un e-mail all'indirizzo info@getty-images.com, indicando l'immagine scelta e il numero di pagina di riferimento.

Hulton Getty Online

Tutte le immagini elencate di seguito e molte altre sono disponibili via Hulton Getty Online all'indirizzo:
http://www.hultongetty.com

Per ottenere gli originali

Per ulteriori informazioni su come acquisire le riproduzioni per le esposizioni contattare The Hulton Getty Picture Gallery, al numero di telefono 00 44 171 376 4525. (fax) +44 171 376 4524 hulton.gallery@getty-images.com

Acknowledgements

Slava Katamidze 278